To Jonathan

Jell Briscoe

Jonah and the Worm

Jonah and the Worm

Jill Briscoe

THOMAS NELSON PUBLISHERS
NASHVILLE · CAMDEN · NEW YORK

Cover and text art by Tom Armstrong and Florence Davis

Copyright © 1983 by Briscoe Ministries

All rights reserved. Written permission must be secured from the publisher to use or reproduce any part of this book, except for brief quotations in critical reviews or articles.

Published in Nashville, Tennessee, by Thomas Nelson, Inc. and distributed in Canada by Lawson Falle, Ltd., Cambridge, Ontario.

Printed in the United States of America.

Scripture quotations are from The New King James Version. Copyright © 1979, 1980, 1982, Thomas Nelson, Inc., Publishers.

Library of Congress Cataloging in Publication Data

Briscoe, Jill.
   Jonah and the worm.

   Summary: A retelling of the Old Testament story of Jonah using worms as the principal characters. Each chapter is followed by discussion questions and suggestions for prayers.
   1. Christian life—1960-   —Juvenile literature.
2. Children—Religious life. [1. Christian life]
I. Title.
BV4515.2.B74   1983   224'.9209505   83-6232
ISBN 0-8407-5289-X

Contents

Preface 7
1. The Pond Party 9
2. The Worker 24
3. The Wind and the Whale 38
4. Town Worm 52
5. Holes 65
6. The Wicked King 77
7. Really, Really, *Really* Sorry 89
8. Early Bird 102
9. Warm Worms and a Weird Weed 114
10. Silk Worm 129

TO MY OWN
CHILDREN

DAVE • JUDY • PETE

FOR WHOM I THANK
GOD
EVERY DAY OF MY LIFE

Preface

The true story of Jonah has been well told by many; yet I consider it such a worthy tale it bears retelling—this time by a most unusual eyewitness—Little Worm by name!

This book was written so that parents may read it to children, or children may read it to parents, or anybody may read it to anybody else who, like the author, is a child at heart!

The *Talk Time* and *Prayer Time* sections at the end of the chapters are provided to give an opportunity for "people time"—quiet points in hurried days when we can look into each other's eyes, listen to what is being said, and apply the truths and morals of the story to our hearts.

The tale of *Jonah and the Worm,* told here as a fantasy married to fact, is to be mixed with faith and laughter, shared with love and joy. I hope you enjoy reading Little Worm's story as much as I enjoyed writing it.

Jill Briscoe

But now ask the beasts,
> and they will teach you;
And the birds of the air,
> and they will tell you;
Or speak to the earth,
> and it will teach you;
And the fish of the sea
> will explain to you.

> Job 12:7–8

1
The Pond Party

The Pond Party had begun before Little Worm arrived. That was not unusual for him. He was so small it took him a long time to go anywhere, and he had been known to miss appointments altogether.

As he wriggled onto a central leaf hanging high above the placid water, he glanced around and noticed that everyone who was "anyone" was there. On his left Greedy Grub gripped a leaf and appeared to be in real danger of tumbling into the Pond. Apparently he had become tired of waiting for the party food to arrive and had started to nibble away his leaf seat.

Thinking ahead to the time when his friend would have to find a cocoon caused Little Worm to sigh. This was going to be especially difficult for Greedy Grub, who was a bit plump, because this year's fall fashions were calling for the slim line.

Glancing to the right, Little Worm's eyes lighted on Grumpy Grub. For once he was smiling, which was quite a shock. No one at the Pond could ever remember seeing anything but a frown on Grumpy Grub's sour face, but somehow he had caught the excitement in the air and seemed glad that he had been invited to the party. Who wanted to be grumpy all the time anyway? Grumpiness made you feel dark and chilly inside.

Little Worm looked around for a sight of the Great Grubs. They were the wise worms of the group, and it was their responsibility to call a Pond Party whenever important business needed attending to. He gasped in delight when he saw them. They were sitting closely together on an almost transparent lime green leaf, their woolly jumpers (it was quite cool at the Pond that day) blending perfectly with the background of the bushes.

"How handsome they are," Little Worm remarked to Grumpy Grub, pointing his nose toward the Great Grubs.

Grumpy Grub nodded grudgingly. He was not used to giving compliments, but he had to admit they looked very handsome indeed.

Suddenly, the leaves rustled and Mother and Father Worm appeared. They waved their antennas in Little Worm's direction but seemed to be in a terrible hurry to give the Great Grubs the strange looking package they carried between them.

"It's a letter from heaven," they shouted excitedly.

All of the worms gasped and gazed at the object, a shiny airmail letter, bright with promise, which had been sealed with a dewdrop from a fine summer morning. The worms began whispering among themselves and soon the Pond was buzzing with excitement. No one could remember ever receiving such a thing. *It was fitting to have called a Pond Party today,* thought Little Worm, *so that everyone can hear the message read together.*

The Pond fairly shimmered with fat grubs and thin grubs, slow worms and fast worms! Even the weak worms had dragged themselves out of their sick beds to see what the commotion was all about. Everyone wormed their way over and round everyone else to get the best possible view of the letter, and they all wondered who it was addressed to. They knew it must have come from the Wonder Maker, but they couldn't imagine why He would want to write to anybody at their little pond.

"Open the letter, open the letter!" shouted Greedy Grub, thinking there might be something good to eat inside.

The Wise Worms shook their heads in despair. No one at their pond had ever learned to read. After all, they were worms for such a short time it hardly seemed a wise use of money to send anyone away to grub school.

"This is really going to pose a problem," whispered Little Worm to Grumpy Grub.

Suddenly, Wisest Worm had an idea. "Why don't we

send for Book Worm? He lives only a pond and a half a pond away, and I've heard he is very learned indeed."

At this Father Worm spoke up shyly, saying he hoped the honorable Great Grubs wouldn't mind but he had already taken the liberty of sending for Book Worm as soon as the letter had arrived. "In fact," he said, "he should be here at any minute."

Sure enough, within a very short time Book Worm appeared. He looked very intelligent indeed. Behind him he dragged a huge pair of eyeglasses with dark green sunshades firmly attached.

"Why does he have sunshades on his glasses?" muttered Greedy Grub to Little Worm.

"I expect it's because he knows the letter is from heaven and may be too bright to read," Little Worm replied.

A sweet calm fell over the entire pond as Book Worm took the Wonder Maker's letter and opened it ever so gently. He adjusted his eyeglasses and cleared his throat, and then in a hushed tone, with the utmost awe, read: "God has prepared a worm."

That was all. Searching the front and back of the letter for some more information, Book Worm could find nothing. There was no address and no signature, in fact, no clues at all. He looked around the pond terribly bewildered. Everyone sat extremely still, thinking about the Wonder Maker's puzzling letter.

Book Worm rubbed an antenna over his forehead and blinked tired eyes behind his huge spectacles. "Who do you think it's for?" he asked at last. "And what do you think it means? Whatever does the Wonder Maker want us to do?"

Wisest Worm stared at the letter. A breeze swept across the Pond and made the water's surface look like rippled sand. Then a gust of wind caught the letter and lifted it up, whirling it into a sunbeam where it tumbled and danced about before spinning away to the other side of the Pond. Everyone watched breathlessly as it began to descend, finally coming to rest at the feet of Little Worm.

The assembly of worms gasped. Book Worm spoke softly into the startled silence. "The letter is for him!" he said, pointing at Little Worm.

The strangest feeling came over Little Worm. *There surely must be some mistake,* he thought. *How could it possibly be for me! Why, I am only a worm, and the littlest worm at that!*

Mother and Father Worm twined their antennas around each other and looked at Little Worm with new respect. "Fancy that, God preparing *our* worm!" Mother said.

Preparing me for what? Little Worm wondered.

Suddenly a murmur of excitement spread through the crowd. Right before their eyes the letter began to

THE POND PARTY

change, folding itself over and over again, growing larger and larger until it became a furry covered ball you could see through—like a clear cocoon! Then tiny silver threads appeared and worked busily, hemming in the edges of the ball and sealing it up. A soft breeze kissed it finished, making the cozy thing look very inviting.

"What am I supposed to do now?" Little Worm asked of no one in particular.

"Maybe you should climb inside and become a butterfly." suggested Greedy Grub, eyeing the luscious looking leaf on which Little Worm sat. Greedy was so hungry he had lost interest in the cocoon and wished the whole affair was over with. But Little Worm wasn't listening to him. He had noticed some words plainly written upon a tiny door on the side of the cocoon.

Meanwhile, all the other grubs had wriggled around the Pond as quickly as they could and were trying to clamber up the side of Little Worm's stalk. The leaf where he was sitting bent precariously over the Pond, and he shouted to them all to get back or they might tumble the precious cocoon right into the water! Book Worm had won the race and had managed to crawl up beside Little Worm. Close behind Book Worm came Little Worm's friend Grubby Grub, who was busy plunking his grubby little feet all over the lovely cocoon.

"Don't do that," Little Worm shouted to him. "If you

go on putting your dirty feet all over the writing, Book Worm will never be able to read the words!"

Grubby Grub sulkily wriggled to the back of the leaf while Book Worm began to read the words on the door of the cocoon. "It says 'Go to Nineveh,'" he reported. "And look," he continued, "the Wonder Maker has drawn a clear map and given instructions for you. The map shows that Nineveh is a great city in the country of Assyria where many wicked people live. It lies to the east, toward the rising of the sun. It's a pond ahead and two ponds to the right. The cocoon is a sort of suitcase and has to be taken along to carry your supplies. The Wonder Maker says that He has spun it for you because the journey will take you an awfully long time and you will be needing all your energies for higher things!"

"Hi-hi-higher things?" Little Worm stammered. "What sort of higher things?"

"You are to leave at once," Book Worm said, reading the instructions intently. "You must say good-bye to your parents, because you will never see them again."

At this Little Worm burst into tears! How could he ever stand it! He couldn't even imagine saying good-bye to his parents forever. There had never been a day that his mother and father had not come by his house to say hello, to leave a leaf paper, and to touch his antennas with theirs in deep affection, reminding him they would be around if he needed them. He couldn't face life without them.

And who would help them climb into their cocoons when the time came? The pond creatures looked forward all their lives to that event—an occasion that was always a grand Pond Party. Little Worm felt better after thinking about this. Saying good-bye to someone you loved with all your heart was hard, but it helped to know that in a while "the change" would take place. The little worn bodies of his parents would be left behind as the Wonder Maker did His miracle and turned them into butterflies.

Little Worm had often sat on his leaf porch and watched the beautiful butterflies who lived around the Pond. He recognized a few of them of course. His aunt Ethel had been "changed" in the spring and had chosen to build her house quite near his. They had always liked each other; in fact she had told him once that he was her favorite nephew. And she had wormed her way into his heart by spinning many a yarn with him at bedtime. Since her "change" he had enjoyed having her living so close, watching a familiar butterfly flutter by.

But he couldn't help it, the more Little Worm thought about leaving his mother and father and his dear aunt Ethel, the sadder he became. He began to cry, huge, salty tears tumbling from his eyes. "Why can't my father and mother go along?" he sobbed.

Just then he had another idea. If his family couldn't go with him, maybe Book Worm could. He wiggled to the learned creature's house and asked him, "How ever will I remember all of my instructions without someone to help me?"

Book Worm, who also had no desire to leave the Pond, did not answer but carefully reread the letter. "You are to go all by yourself," he exclaimed, looking very relieved. "The Wonder Maker Himself has promised to go with you," he assured Little Worm, "so you needn't worry about being left all alone."

"It seems a bit unfair of the Wonder Maker to expect him to do it all by himself," remarked Grumpy Grub, who had been listening in.

Wisest Worm looked disapprovingly at Grumpy and reminded him what the letter said—how the Wonder Maker had "prepared the Little Worm." "That means He must have prepared him to be able to be lonely," he said. "Everyone knows the Wonder Maker would never ask anyone to do anything without giving him the needed strength."

Grumpy Grub looked ashamed and tried to pretend that Greedy Grub had made the silly remark.

"There is one last thing written here at the tip of the cocoon," Book Worm said. He held the cocoon near his squinting eyes. "It's in the smallest of letters and says—'Will you go for me?'"

THE POND PARTY

"Will I go?" stammered Little Worm. "You mean I have a choice?"

"Apparently you do," Book Worm said, smiling.

Little Worm was totally confused. To be prepared by the Wonder Maker for some important task was one thing; but to leave his pond, his mother and father, the wise worms, and all his friends—that was quite another. It certainly would be easier if he hadn't been given a choice! *Why doesn't the Wonder Maker just make me do it?* he wondered. *That way He would be sure the job, whatever it is, would get done.*

As if he were reading his thoughts, Book Worm said quietly, "The Wonder Maker wants you to *want* to do it."

Oh dear, thought Little Worm. *Now whatever should I do?* He wanted so very much to *want* to do it, but no matter how hard he tried to feel good about it, he just didn't! He decided he'd better pray. "Oh, dear Wonder Maker," he began timidly, "I'm sorry my feelings don't want me to go, but please help me to go anyway. Perhaps, if my feelings discover they're not going to stop me, they may catch up and come along."

High in heaven the Wonder Maker smiled. His littlest worm was learning fast, discovering that you don't always feel like doing the right thing but you should do it anyway.

Just then Little Worm had another thought. This time it was a very frightening one. "What—what about

Early Bird?" he asked Greedy Grub in sudden panic. "Everybody knows that Early Bird *always* gets the worm!"

"You'll just have to set off before Early Bird gets up," snapped Greedy Grub. He was so ravenous by now he had begun to chew on his toenails. He was worried that Little Worm would never make up his mind so they could have dinner.

Little Worm sat absolutely still, frozen with fear at the very idea of Early Bird. Terrible pictures flashed into his mind. He imagined the huge glistening body of his enemy, with black wings outspread and that sharp orange beak pointing straight at him, hurtling down from the sky to gobble him up.

The Wonder Maker spoke from heaven with a voice like a million waterfalls. "Little Worm," He said, "remember I live in the heavens too. I will take care of Early Bird. I will keep you in the right way. If you are willing to do My will, you will find Me willing to be your shield!"

"Well, now, that's good news," said Mother Worm to Father Worm with great relief.

"Will Little Worm go?" croaked one frog to another. "Will he leave his mother and his father?" a leaf rustled on a tall tree. "Will he obey the Wonder Maker?" whispered an old wise worm to another.

Little Worm's mother watched him tenderly. He

THE POND PARTY

seemed so very, very small to be making such an important choice on his own. Big tears splashed from her eyes down on her little black feet and fell into the pond like rain. She remembered the day he had been born, so absolutely perfect, but oh, so very, very, small. He had been the smallest baby at the Pond. She had worried about him because just being a worm was hard, but being the very *littlest* worm would be harder still. She had prayed to the Wonder Maker for help to raise him properly and that he, though weeny, would become a wise worm.

"Never in our history has God prepared a worm to do His work," commented Book Worm wonderingly.

"Go, little one!" called out all the pond creatures in chorus.

Little Worm looked up into the sky. Was it his imagination or did he see the Wonder Maker smiling down at him? It seemed he did, and suddenly that was enough. *After all, God appointed me, even if I'm just a worm, and little is much then!* he thought. "I'll go!" he cried.

The worms cheered and the Pond Party began in earnest. Food was served on the big lily leaves that floated on Little Worm's beloved pond, and everyone began celebrating Little Worm's decision. Greedy Grub was the happiest of all. Now at last he could eat his dinner.

Later that night supplies and other necessary articles were loaded into the heavenly cocoon. Some frozen food was dug up from last winter's cold storage. Someone found a photo of Little Worm's parents on their wedding day. Grumpy Grub even gave Little Worm a red bandanna for his head in case the sun became too hot. Little Worm was touched. He didn't want to take the bandanna from Grumpy Grub, because He knew his friend used it to wrap around his head when he got a headache. Grumpy had many headaches, because grumpiness always hurts your head!

Silk Worm wriggled up to Little Worm and shyly offered him three pairs of beautiful blue silk running shoes that she had been spinning for the cross-country team. "They will help you to speed over the ground to Nineveh," she said quietly. Silk Worm was very, very sad to see Little Worm go. She had secret hopes that they might hold antennas one romantic moonlit night and maybe share a cozy cocoon in the future. It had been a long time since the Pond had celebrated a worm wedding! *It's not an easy thing to do the Wonder Maker's will,* Silk Worm thought. *It affects so many lives.*

Finally, at a very late hour, Grubby Grub hoisted the cocoon onto Little Worm's back. Mother and Father Worm wrapped their antennas tightly around him and then wordlessly sent him on his wiggly way.

"Go to Nineveh," the Wonder Maker had said. So Little Worm obeyed. The Great Adventure had begun!

THE POND PARTY

Talk Time

1. What were the names of Little Worm's friends?
2. Why did Little Worm feel there had been some mistake when he received the Wonder Maker's letter?
3. Why didn't Little Worm want to go to Nineveh?
4. What did Little Worm learn about his feelings?

Prayer Time

Pray that you will be obedient even when you *don't* feel like it.

2
The Worker

A pond to the right and two ponds beyond, the Worker lay on the grassy bank of a swift-flowing stream. Dawdling his hand in the water, he watched several tiny fish dart around looking for food in the depths among the reeds. Now and then, one of them would turn and struggle frantically in the heavy current, trying to swim against the flow.

"Any old fish can swim with the stream," mused the Worker, "but it takes a lively one to swim against it!" The Worker picked up a small twig and flipped it casually into the water. The current whisked it away. *Serving the Wonder Maker is a bit like swimming upstream,* he thought. *All the fish around you seem to be flowing along with the tide, which is by far the easiest thing to do. Swimming in the opposite direction is much harder and can be pretty lonely, too.*

Thinking about it all made the Worker weary, so he gave a great sigh. His people, called the Israelites, knew the Wonder Maker and His ways and had tried to follow

Him. Sometimes they got tired, though, as other people nearby served other gods and were always trying to persuade them to do the same thing. *Doing the will of the Wonder Maker makes you feel like a fish swimming against the stream,* the Worker thought. He stopped playing in the water and rolled onto his back so he could see the sky.

High in a tree above the Worker, Early Bird was waking up, preparing for the day's adventures. The creature opened his beak and warbled a shrill song, all the while shaking his black, shiny feathers, dusting himself, and darting quick glances downward—looking for fat little worms for breakfast! He was a bit tired today. His wings ached from flying long and hard the day before.

Some time ago Early Bird had heard a rumor that special gourmet worms could be found in Assyria, a neighboring country, so yesterday he had set off to see. If he had known how far away Assyria was he wouldn't have gone, but the thought of foreign food had spurred him on, so he had flown long and high until eventually he'd arrived in the strange country.

It had been a very disappointing trip. Instead of cool forest streams and reeds and an abundance of food, he had found a hot, dusty city, and oh, so many, many noisy people! Everyone rushed here and there shouting at everyone else. He had seen some prison guards whipping a prisoner and some children beating a dog to death. The Assyrian Army was drilling for a big war somewhere, and one of the soldiers had thrown a sharp jagged stone straight at Early Bird. That had been enough. Turning around, he had flown away as fast and as high as he could, back to his nest in the cool forest glade.

No wonder, then, that his wings felt stiff this morning and his feathers needed washing. He flew down to the stream to have a bath, and seeing the Worker lying on the bank of the stream, decided to tell him the whole story. The Worker listened very carefully to all that Early Bird said. A very, very angry look crossed the Worker's face, and noticing this, Early Bird decided it would be better not to wait around in case another stone was thrown in his direction! Hastily ruffling out his feathers, he fluttered back to his treetop home, awakened Mrs. Early Bird, and told her to get up and find him some breakfast.

The Worker lay very still thinking about all that Early Bird had said. He was worried about the Assyrians. They were a fierce people who had conquered everyone who lived around them. Now he realized they were getting ready to invade his country. He wondered what the Wonder Maker thought about it all. He couldn't be pleased with the cruelty of the Assyrians. The

THE WORKER   27

Worker hoped that they would be stopped and decided to pray about it: "Oh Wonder Maker," he said, "please save us."

Suddenly the Wonder Maker Himself appeared on the river bank and sat down quietly beside the Worker. "I have heard your prayer," He said in the voice that sounded like a million waterfalls.

The Worker gasped with surprise, fell down on his face, and worshiped the Wonder Maker. The Worker was delighted to know that his prayers were heard. He couldn't wait to hear what was going to happen. Perhaps the Wonder Maker would send a whirlwind to carry the Ninevites off into the desert where they all would be buried in the sand. Or maybe He would cause a flood to sweep over the earth and drown them all, like He had done in Noah's day. Then again, He might even speak to the ground and command it to open its mouth and swallow them all up. He didn't know how the wicked men of Nineveh would be destroyed, but he was sure the Wonder Maker would find just the right way.

He got quite a shock, therefore, when the Wonder Maker said to him: "Get up and go to Nineveh! Tell those who live in that great city that they must repent; I know how wicked they are!"

The Worker was speechless. *Go to Nineveh?* he thought. *How could he possibly be expected to do that? And what would be the point anyway? Why, the people there were so evil they would never listen to him—even if he did go. Anyway, he didn't want to leave his country, his mother and his father, and all his friends. The journey would be far too dangerous. No, he wasn't going to be foolish enough to go to Nineveh!*

The Worker's thoughts were stopped short when the Wonder Maker asked, "Will you go for Me?"

"You mean I have a choice?" the Worker replied, suddenly hopeful.

"You are free to obey Me, and you are free to disobey Me. I won't force you to do what I ask you to do."

"Well, that's good," said the Worker, highly relieved. He jumped up hurriedly and ran off into the forest as fast as he could go, in case the Wonder Maker changed His mind. He ran and he ran as hard as he could away from the stream, away from Nineveh, and away from the Wonder Maker. Knowing that there was a boat at Joppa that would take him to the town of Tarshish at the opposite end of the country, he headed in that direction. Unknown to him, the Worker now raced away from Nineveh on the very same trail Little Worm was taking through the forest to Nineveh.

In heaven a pair of angels were watching the whole scene. "Now that is an amazing sight," one angel commented. "Just look at Little Worm hurrying toward Nineveh as fast as his little feet—clad in all those silk running shoes—will take him. And just listen to the

Worker's feet drumming a dance of defiant disobedience as he runs away in the opposite direction!"

Flying along the path the Worker narrowly missed stepping on Little Worm's wobbly body and squashing him quite flat as he pounded over his head! "Who—whoever was that?" Little Worm gulped in dismay, shaking all over at his narrow escape. He had been so intent on watching the path he hadn't noticed the big feet racing toward him, even when the ground had begun to shake.

"That was my Worker," said the Wonder Maker, who suddenly appeared and knelt beside Little Worm, gently wiping the perspiration away from the little creature's eyes. "He doesn't want to go to Nineveh!"

Goodness me, thought Little Worm, *is everyone in the whole wide world going to Nineveh? Wouldn't it be awfully crowded once they all arrived?* "Why is he running in the opposite direction?" he timidly inquired of the Wonder Maker.

"He doesn't like Ninevites" was the answer.

Little Worm wanted to say that he didn't think he was going to like them very much either, but he didn't dare. "Did your Worker have a choice about going?" he asked in a very small voice.

"Of course," answered the Wonder Maker. "Everybody has a choice."

"It makes it awfully hard for us," ventured the little

THE WORKER 31

creature. "I mean, if the thing that you have given us to do is a very hard thing, it would be easier if you made us do it, rather than letting us decide!"

"Whoever told you that obedience was supposed to be easy?" the Wonder Maker inquired gravely.

"No one, no one" answered Little Worm hastily, continuing on his way. He wondered about the Worker and why he was running away from Nineveh. *You can't just run away from people you don't like,* Little Worm thought. *That's silly. There're bound to be some people everywhere you don't get along with. Why, maybe the Worker would get to Tarshish and find out he didn't like the people who lived there either! Little Worm felt very sad about it all.*

Little Worm had glimpsed the Worker's face as he fled past and noticed how awfully tired he looked. That was funny, because the man's legs were dozens of inches longer than all of Little Worm's put together; and yet Little Worm didn't feel tired at all. In fact, he felt full of energy! Did obedience lend strength to your feet?

Maybe the Worker had just become tired of doing the Wonder Maker's will. After all, prophets were human, too. Perhaps he was just a pooped prophet! Or then again, it could be he was suffering from sheer fright! *After all,* thought the little crawling creature, shivering at the idea, *the Wonder Maker has probably told his servant to go and tell the nasty Ninevites how very nasty they are.* Then Little Worm was gripped by a terrible thought: *Perhaps the Wonder Maker was sending him to take the Worker's place!* But to Little Worm's relief, as fast as the thought had appeared, it disappeared. It really had been quite a ridiculous idea. Worms didn't preach, everybody knew that! God must have something very different in mind for him.

Little Worm wriggled along his way. Turning his head to look behind him, he saw the Wonder Maker in the distance following the Worker. Little Worm wondered what was going to happen. Maybe the Wonder Maker would try to persuade the disobedient helper to change his mind.

Little Worm's musing was interrupted once more. The two angels, wanting to encourage him, patted him on the head and told him he was doing a fine job. "Press on and do not worry about the Worker," one of them said cheerily. As they left him he heard the other beautiful angelic being say, "What a thing is this! Little Worm obeys, and yet the Worker doesn't."

Little Worm felt a warm glow spreading all over his body. It started at the tip of his head and traveled right down to his toes (and there were a lot of them to travel to). It took an awful lot of glow to go around but there was enough. The warm feeling was the joy of doing the Wonder Maker's will, but of course Little Worm didn't know that yet. He had always supposed that joy was

THE WORKER

happiness, and that happiness depended on happenings. If your happenings happened to happen the way you happened to want them to happen, then you'd be happy!

Now Little Worm was learning that joy was different. Joy was happiness when nothing was happening right! Humming a little tune he fairly sped over the ground. Glancing down at his feet clad in the beautiful blue silk running shoes that Silk Worm had spun for him, he smiled. *Why, if I get enough practice I might be able to enter the cross-country races at the next Worms' Field Day,* he thought. But swiftly on the heels of that bright idea followed the words that Book Worm had read to him off the side of the cocoon. "You will never see your father or mother again." "Well," he said to himself, "it didn't say I'd never see Silk Worm or Greedy, Grubby, or Grumpy Grub again!"

Cheered by this thought, he decided to stop for some food and lowered the cocoon carefully onto the ground. He thought that his shoulder would be rubbed raw by now, carrying such a big thing around for such a long time, but it wasn't. Somehow he seemed to remember the Wonder Maker saying that "the burden He asked you to bear would be easy and light." This had certainly been true so far.

Opening the door of the cocoon he reached inside and felt about for something to eat. He found a huge sandwich and a little knife that in an enchanting fashion opened itself in the shape of a warm summer smile. Glinting in the sun, the knife used its little metal foot to skate across the sandwich and slice it clean in half, then in half again and again until the food lay in bite-size pieces.

How kind of Grinny Grub to make me a sandwich, thought Little Worm. Grinny was a cheerful baker-worm who lived at the far end of the Pond. He was a kind grub, always helping others. No doubt it was he who had put the big king-size sandwich into the cocoon.

Little Worm thanked the knife for its help, whereupon it vanished. Startled, Little Worm looked around for it, but after awhile decided it would come back when necessary, so he might as well settle down to eat his sandwich. He was hungry, and knowing he had a long, hard day's walk in front of him, Little Worm saved only two pieces for a snack along the way.

Little Worm was patting his stomach when a clean white napkin floated out from the door of the cocoon. "Have you finished?" it asked, in a flutterly sort of voice.

"Yes, thank you," replied Little Worm. He was now quite used to strange things happening! The napkin tiptoed over to him on thin, papery feet, began to twirl around, unwrapped itself, and finally engulfed Little Worm, patting the butter off his mouth, mopping the jam off his whiskers and wiping his little nose—all at once! Rolling itself up into a ball, the napkin then tumbled down the river bank into a hole so it wouldn't litter the pathway.

"Thank you," murmured Little Worm gratefully. He lapped a drink from the cool stream, then picked up the cocoon and set off again toward Nineveh.

Little Worm marched down the path, on the strength of that food, an hour and four more before he felt like stopping again. He had covered a huge distance, and he was actually happy when dusk appeared, warning him of the dark night that lay ahead. Little Worm liked dusk. Nothing was absolutely black when it was around. You could still see familiar faces and everything turned a sort of pretty pink. He remembered how beautiful Silk Worm looked whenever dusk came and wondered with a little stab of homesickness if she were blushing. "Well," he said to himself sternly, "it's no good thinking about Silk Worm now; I'd better start thinking about tonight!"

It was quite dark by now. Little Worm began to wonder if he'd better stop and rest, even though he felt strong enough to walk a few more miles. He was really worried about traveling in the dark. His father and mother had always told him it was very dangerous to be alone at such times. There were many enemies who only came out in the woods at night and were especially on the lookout for juicy little worms like him who should be at home and in bed.

But walking in the woods at night wasn't as bad as

he had feared. Somehow the path was strangely lit around him. He could see everything he needed to see and, in fact, he felt as though he were traveling within a small pool of light like a miniature spotlight—which indeed he was!

Unknown to him, the warm flush of happiness from the joy of doing the Wonder Maker's will had filled his whole body with the soft sweet light. A miracle had happened! The Wonder Maker had marvelously prepared His little worm for the job he was to do. You see, Little Worm had been created to glow in order to produce his own light. The darker the night became, the brighter his little body would glow. "I never thought it would be possible to do God's will in the dark!" Little Worm said softly.

"Obedience lights up the darkness with rays of radiance," whispered one of the angels who had come back to make sure everything was under control.

Little Worm had heard many stories about glowworms but he had never realized he was one of them. Because his mother and father had never allowed him to go out at night, he had never found out he could glow in the dark. He grew really excited. Being so small didn't seem to matter as much if he could only bring a pinprick of light into the darkness. Now he could see the path and would not fall into any pot holes. *Walking along this path in these quiet woods on a lovely evening is really a cheerful place to be,* he thought. The light

THE WORKER

shut out the strange and frightening shadows that loomed on either side of him.

"Oh Wonder Maker," he said. "why did you never tell me I was a glowworm?"

The Wonder Maker laughed, "Sometimes you never know what you can do until the darkness falls around you," He said. "Walk on now, carefully, Little Worm. You need to cover a few more miles before you rest."

Meanwhile, at that very moment, the Worker arrived at the port city of Joppa and persuaded the captain of a ship going to Tarshish to take him on board. He paid the captain a lot of money for his ticket. After walking up the vessel's gangplank, the Worker went down into the lowest hold of the ship where he collapsed upon the bare boards. Totally exhausted, he fell into a deep and troubled sleep.

Talk Time

1. What sort of a worm was Little Worm?
2. Is being obedient easy?
3. Why do you think the Wonder Maker gives us a choice about obeying Him?

Prayer Time

Pray about something 'hard' you need to do this week.

3
The Wind and the Whale

Early the next morning, while the Worker still slept in the bottom of the ship, Little Worm set off again along the forest path to Nineveh.

Feeling a little lonely, he stopped for a moment to rummage through the cocoon and find the photograph of his mother and father on their wedding day. Looking at their happy faces made him feel even more homesick, so he put the picture away and started to sing himself a little song instead. He didn't have a very good voice, in fact he could only sing one note, but that was better than nothing. And, as his father always said, "God hears the crows as well as the nightingales."

The birds were not awake yet to embarrass Little Worm with their beautiful morning music, so he felt quite free to express himself. But with his first thought of *birds,* Little Worm's body contorted in fright. Distracted by his loneliness he had quite forgotten about Early Bird. He wondered how "early" Early Bird got up? No one had ever given him that piece of information. He only knew that Early Bird was his enemy because back at the Pond, Wise Worm had warned everyone to watch out for him. Little Worm had spent many days building underground air-raid shelters for his family, in case Early Bird dived at them. Little Worm had to remind himself that as surely as the Wonder Maker had prepared him for a special task, He would just as surely protect him from his enemies.

For a long time the only sounds in the forest were the noises of the night creatures coming home from work and retiring for the day. Little Worm had stopped singing, afraid that he might wake Early Bird up. He tried to think of pleasanter things

(5) After rounding a curve in the path, Little Worm abruptly halted—strangely aware of something different—a presence nearby. The feeling was really eerie, and he turned his head this way and that, trying to see who or what was near him. His antennas stood straight up on his little head in fright, for he couldn't see anyone! His fear grew—someone was very, very near to him. Little Worm actually felt a heavy breath on his cheek.

"Hello-o-o," said a sort of "whooey" voice out of nowhere. Squirming in shock, Little Worm frantically searched the shrubs around him to see who had spoken. He saw nothing—nothing, that is, except the branches of trees swaying to and fro and the tall grass bending down like the reeds beside his beloved Pond. The memory of the Pond immediately reminded him of home and made him quite homesick all over again.

"Who-o-o are yooou?" asked the unseen visitor.

"I'm Little Worm," he whispered in the littlest voice. "God has appointed me to go to Nineveh," he added bravely, hoping the unseen voice would know that this was one worm who wasn't to be tampered with. No response came, so Little Worm shakily asked the invisible whooey voice, "Who are . . . who are you?" He still searched for a sight of his unseen companion.

"I am the w-w-w-w-wind!" came the answer.

Then Little Worm understood why he had felt the breath upon his cheek and why the trees and grasses were moving about. No wonder he couldn't see anyone, for who has ever seen the Wind?

"The Wonder Maker has appointed me to do some work for Him," the Wind informed him, blowing a beautiful crimson butterfly awake.

"Are you going to Nineveh, too?" Little Worm asked excitedly.

"Well, yes and no-o-o," replied the Wind.

Little Worm was puzzled and a little disappointed. He felt awfully lonely again.

"I'm go-o-o-oing to go to the seaside fir-r-r-rst," the Wind explained further.

"Well, that's nice," said Little Worm. "But what are you to do there?"

"I am to pla-a-a-a-a-y with the wa-a-a-a-ves. The Wonder Maker has allowed me to have a part in cha-a-a-sing the ship that carries His Worker to Tarshi-i-i-i-sh."

"However will you do that?" gasped Little Worm.

"Oh, it will be a bree-e-e-e-ze," wheezed the Wind, chuckling. "I have to go-o-o-o-o now tho-o-o-o-o-gh," he finished, puffing some pesky flies away from Little Worm's head. "I've stayed to-o-o-o-o long already, so I'd better be on my wa-a-a-y. My wife, the Whirlwind, alwa-a-a-a-ys says I'm just an old windba-a-a-g." With that the kiss of the Wind's breath vanished, and the leaves were still again on the branches. The grasses stood straight and tall, touching the tips of the sunbeams, greeting them with the promise of a new day.

Little Worm sighed and crawled on his way. He was hungry again, and so he wriggled his way over a stick and stopped to nibble a tasty leaf. The Wonder Maker appeared from nowhere, giving Little Worm quite a start. He carried cold water in His heavenly hand, beautifully cupped in half an acorn. A rose petal was neatly folded over the cup to keep dust out. Little Worm drank deeply and, feeling refreshed, set off up the path. He couldn't help but wonder secretly why the Wonder Maker had told the Wind what to do but had not bothered to tell him! The task might seem so much easier if he knew what lay ahead.

Little Worm sighed once more and hardly noticed the snake that slithered in front of him, blocking the path. The snake put his flat, oval-shaped head near Little Worm's face and hissed: "Maybe the Wonder Maker hasn't told you your mission because it's bad news. He doesn't want to frighten you off!"

Now Little Worm knew all about snakes. That was how all the trouble had started in the first place. If it hadn't been for the serpent's tricks beside the Wonder Maker's very first pond, there wouldn't have been any wicked Assyrians doing evil things. Little Worm knew that listening to the snake wouldn't help at all, so he didn't say a word and brushed past the snake as if he weren't even there.

In anger the snake coiled his body and slithered back in front of Little Worm again. "The Wonder Maker is taking you to Nineveh because He wants to feed you to the big birds that live there," he hissed with wicked glee. "That's why He hasn't told you what you are to do once you get there!"

Little Worm tried not to listen. He stopped and put the cocoon down on the pathway between himself and the snake. Opening the tiny door he looked inside for something to help him. He saw the bandanna Grumpy Grub had given him in case the hot sun made his head hurt. *Why, that would be ideal!* he thought. He hurriedly pulled the large handkerchief out and tied it around his head, carefully covering his ears. Now he couldn't hear the sly old snake anymore.

Little Worm knew he looked a bit funny—two squirrels dropped their nuts in amazement as he wriggled past them—but he didn't care. Who cared what he looked like anyway, as long as he couldn't hear the sly old snake's snide remarks? The sight of Little Worm, with his three pairs of blue silk running shoes on his feet and a gay red bandanna tied around his head, struck the snake as very amusing, and he started to hiss with laughter. By the time he stopped laughing, Little Worm had turned the corner.

Suddenly, Little Worm heard a loud swish and a whir of wings. He glanced skyward and saw Early Bird level out, then head down in a screaming dive straight at the scarey snake, chasing him right out of sight. Early Bird hadn't seemed to notice Little Worm, who shivered in fear and scrambled under a pine cone. *I guess if God elects you, He protects you,* Little Worm reflected.

By the time the Wind arrived at Joppa the Worker's ship was far out to sea. Since he was a little bit late, the Wind was relieved to find the Wonder Maker still standing on the seashore waiting for him. After picking the Wind up and telling him to hold his breath, the Wonder Maker drew back His almighty arm and hurled the Wind across the surface of the sea in the direction of the little ship that bobbed along on the horizon.

The Wind landed in the ocean not far from target, and laughing wildly, began to play with the Waves. The Waves had been asleep and it took a little while to wake them up properly, but soon they were having a grand time with the Wind. The watery ruckus was just the sort of thing the Wonder Maker had in mind. The Worker's ship began to toss and turn, pitching and rocking and shaking everybody in it. All the sailors began to throw the cargo overboard, and the Waves—thinking this was great fun—licked hungrily up the sides of the ship for more.

The captain came down into the bottom of the ship where the Worker was snoozing while the storm howled. He shook the man awake and told him he'd better get up and call upon his God and ask Him to stop the terrible storm. Everyone else was praying to their gods, and the captain was amazed that the Worker wasn't praying as well. But then the captain didn't know the Worker was not talking to his God, and was in fact running away from Him.

Climbing up onto the deck the Worker looked around him. When he saw the Wind and the Waves and glanced up into the angry sky, he knew exactly what was happening. He understood that the Wonder Maker had found him and knew that the storm was all his fault. *If you run away from God, you always cause trouble for others,* he thought guiltily, watching the poor sailors trying to control the bucking ship.

Soon the sailors stopped trying to balance the craft and gathered around him. They knew he was running away from the Wonder Maker because he had told them so, and so they asked him what they could do to make the storm stop.

"Take me up and throw me into the sea," the Worker told them, but the men had kind hearts and didn't want to do that. They tried again as hard as they could to sail the ship safely back to shore, but the Wind howled and the Waves waved. The sailors could see there was no way they were going to save themselves.

In the end they picked up the Worker and threw him over the side of the ship just as he had told them to, and at once the Wind ran back to the Wonder Maker on the seashore and the Waves went back to sleep. In amazement the sailors fell down on their faces and praised the Wonder Maker, vowing they would serve Him forever.

As soon as he hit the water, the Worker sank down, down, down, right to the bottom of the sea!

Now the Wonder Maker wasn't finished with the Worker yet and had prepared a "whale" of a surprise! There were many fish in the ocean, but none so great as the Whale. He had a tiny brain, but a huge body and a very big heart. He was a kind mammal and was sorry that the little fish in the sea swam away from him in fright, as he really wanted to play with them. He liked nothing better than a good frolic at the surface of the water on a fine calm day, and so when he had received the invitation to a fish festival earlier that day, he had been delighted. True, it had seemed a bit "fishy" that the invitation had not been signed and no one seemed to know who was throwing the party, but he had decided to go and have a great time anyway.

When he arrived at the party he noticed that everyone that was a really big fish had been invited. There were no small fry around the place at all. A shark sidled up and whispered through his teeth that the Wonder Maker had sent out the invitations and instructed everyone not to eat anything at all for a whole day and night beforehand; He was preparing some very special foreign food for them. The Whale had already eaten a ton of fish, but his stomach was so huge he could always eat a ton more! In fact he became very hungry just hearing all the talk about food.

The big fish thrashed the water with their gigantic tails and made the sea boil like a caldron. But where was the food? They began to wonder if they had mistaken the Wonder Maker's words. Some of the monsters weren't very amused, as they were awfully hungry.

"It's a bit strange," said a sharp-looking shark to a barracuda. "Maybe it's all a hoax."

"No, I don't think so," chipped in a dolphin. "I distinctly heard that there would be a gourmet meal prepared for us."

"Well, where is it then?" asked an impatient porpoise leaping out of the water to scan the surface for food. The angry shark, diving around, bumping into everyone in his selfish haste to have the first bite, swam off into the darkness of the depths with the barracuda at his side. The porpoise began to chase another snappy shark, and suddenly the only fish left around was the big Whale who had been the last to arrive. Flipping his flippers and sending a huge spout of water high above the surface, the huge mammal swam lazily in a gentle circle. The droning signals of his companions' voices soon died away, and the water around him became very still once more.

He dived down to the very bottom of the sea to learn if anything was going on down there. He had noticed that the Waves were churning high above his head, the sign of a terrible storm on the surface of the sea, but here in the depths all was quiet and still.

Suddenly, the Whale blinked as the brightest light he'd ever seen shone right into his eyes. He bowed his big head and worshiped, for he instantly recognized the presence of the Wonder Maker. The Whale couldn't believe his great good fortune—why he couldn't wait to tell all his friends what they'd missed by running off! He was so glad he could thank the Wonder Maker in person for the grand gift of life and the marvelous ocean to swim around in. He wanted to thank the Wonder Maker, too, for feeding and caring for him. In fact the Whale's big old soft heart nearly burst with joy just to be this near to his Maker.

The Wonder Maker smiled at Whale and then wrote some whale words with His finger in the sand on the sea bottom. The big fish moved his huge bulk nearer the letters, and with great curiosity read what the Wonder Maker had written. "Go to Nineveh," the top line of the message said. And then in very small letters underneath was a single word—"Now!" That was all.

Before the Whale had time to think about it there was a huge commotion above him and the strangest fish he'd ever seen appeared right in front of his eyes. The unusual creature had no flippers and was thrashing around, jerking and jumping this way and that. He didn't smell very appetizing, but with some strange instinct the Whale knew that this was "his fish" and that the Wonder Maker wanted him to swallow it whole! By this time he was so hungry that he really didn't care who or what he ate, so the Whale opened his colossal mouth and gulped down the Worker!

The bright light disappeared, and the Whale wondered what he should do next. Before long, the strangest sensation came over him. *It must be that strange fish I've just swallowed,* he thought to himself. He began to lose all sense of direction (You know how you feel when you get sick at your stomach, don't you?). Go to Nine-

veh, the Wonder Maker had said. *Well, maybe He told me to do that because there is a hospital there,* the Whale thought. *I'd better try to swim toward the great city and see if someone can help me there.*

He moved along unsteadily for many miles—in fact he lost all sense of time, not realizing how long his journey was taking. He swam for three days and nights in the direction of Nineveh and by the third day felt so ill he didn't even notice that the water was becoming shallower and shallower. He looked awfully funny, as he was now a delicate shade of green.

"I didn't know doing the will of the Wonder Maker would make me feel so sick or look so funny," Whale grunted to himself. He really felt terrible. The funny fish he had hungrily swallowed was definitely the very worst meal he had ever, ever had. He couldn't seem to digest the thing; it stayed like a dead weight in his stomach. He could actually feel a tickling sensation, like a scratching inside his tummy, when the strange thing moved about.

Floating along in the shallows, the Whale realized he had reached the very shoreline of the sea. And he knew he was going to be sick! How embarrassing it all was. He hadn't known that doing the will of the Wonder Maker could be embarrassing too! Was he ever glad his friends couldn't see him now. With one good, big heave the Whale spit the funny fish up from his stomach right out on the sand, and then it was all over.

A huge joy filled the big empty hole inside the great fish, and suddenly the bright light returned, and the Wonder Maker said, "Well done, good and faithful Whale." The sick feeling was gone, and seeing a school of the most appetizing appetizers just in front of his nose, the Whale swallowed the fish hastily. He smiled at the Wonder Maker, then lumbered off to find his friends and tell them the whole incredible story.

Talk Time

1. Why was Little Worm frightened of Early Bird?
2. Who was the new friend Little Worm met?
3. What enemies do we have that try to stop us from obeying God? What friends do we have that help us?

Prayer Time

Pray for God's protection when you are afraid.

4
Town Worm

The Worker lay on the sand and pinched himself to make sure he wasn't dreaming. He couldn't believe he was still alive. Shuddering, he watched the back of the big fish disappearing into the deeper waters of the sea. How grateful he was to the Wonder Maker that he hadn't drowned when the sailors threw him overboard.

The trip inside the big mammal had been absolutely horrible . . . After being swallowed, the Worker realized he was not dead, but he was filled with a great terror. He began to cry out in pain and fear. Because it was quite dark, he couldn't see anything at all. He kept bumping up against bits of leftover dinner from the Whale's last meal! The big floppy stomach was cold, smelly, and clammy inside, but because the Wonder Maker had made sure the big fish hadn't eaten much beforehand, there was plenty of air.

As the Worker cried out he wondered if the Wonder Maker could hear him? After all he was way down deep at the bottom of the sea. And he had been so disobedient, he didn't expect any help from heaven. As soon as he started to pray however, he felt quite different—but then you *always* do, you know! Not knowing quite what to say, he remembered some verses he'd learned from the Psalms and said them out loud.

This made him feel so much better he decided to go on praying—not the easiest thing to do in a whale's belly. Usually, when he prayed he could lie down flat on his face on a grassy bank, or kneel beside a rock, or stand on top of a broad mountain overlooking some of the Wonder Maker's marvelous creation. But now he was being thrown around this way and that in the pitch black darkness, sometimes even standing upside down on his head. He bumped into the Whale's hard rib cage and felt spiney, half-digested fish hitting him in the face. But the more he prayed the better he began to feel about everything.

The Worker had lost all sense of time, and he didn't dare go to sleep; he was afraid he'd drown if the Whale swallowed some water.

For three days and nights the Worker tumbled about in that dreadful place while the big fish wound its unsteady way toward Nineveh. By the end of that time the Worker had made his peace with the Wonder Maker, and the Worker was conscious of his dear Maker's presence right beside him. The Worker came to understand that there is nothing in heaven, or on earth, or even under the sea that can separate us from the Wonder Maker and stop Him from helping us when we need Him. Why, the Worker was even able to *thank* Him for being kept alive. *It's better to be in the belly of a whale with the Wonder Maker than safe on dry land without Him!* he thought.

Since the Worker couldn't see what was happening, he didn't know when the big fish arrived at the shoreline. The Wonder Maker spoke to His "special submarine," and the big mammal's stomach muscles squeezed the Worker upward—along with everything else inside him! Suddenly the Worker was deposited safely in the shallow waters on the shore.

The Worker splashed to the dry sand, and after flinging himself face downward, he worshiped the Wonder Maker. He was beside himself with joy, for he had survived his ordeal!

After a long, long time, he looked up and saw that the Whale was far out to sea and that the Wonder Maker now stood in front of him. "Go to Nineveh," He said, in the voice that sounded like a million waterfalls.

Oh, no, not again, thought the Worker, *not that*! But he didn't say anything out loud, because by this time he had had quite enough of the consequences of disobedience. He reminded himself that the Wonder Maker didn't need to give him a second chance and could have gone back to Israel and appointed another more willing and obedient prophet to do His work. Looking into his Savior's eyes, he began to understand that the Wonder Maker was just as interested in him as He was in the Ninevites.

As if He had read his thoughts, the Wonder Maker nodded, smiled at him, and said: "You're right; I love My workers who love Me, just as much as I love My world that doesn't! I'm concerned about them both. I don't like to see anyone unhappy."

Then the Worker finally understood why his hard and stubborn heart needed changing just as much as the heart of any wicked person in Nineveh. They both needed forgiveness for their sinfulness.

"When you were in the fish's stomach you asked Me for a *second* chance," the Wonder Maker said quite sternly. "You promised you would pay your vows—remember?"

The Worker remembered alright. Years ago he had vowed he would obediently serve the Wonder Maker and do whatever He asked. Hastily rising to his feet, he splashed into the water to wash himself, and then straightening his wet and somewhat ragged clothes, he set off towards Nineveh. He had no idea how he would preach to the wicked people of that great city, but decided he would worry about that when he got there. The Wonder Maker had promised to tell him exactly what he had to say, so he put it out of his mind. He hurried along, and after traveling for a long, long time, fell down under a scrub bush and slept the soundest sleep possible.

Meanwhile, Little Worm arrived at a bend in the path, and wriggling around it, stopped in amazement. Before him lay wavy sand dunes with scrubby little shrubs sticking out of them like bushy umbrellas. Beyond the sand dunes towered a huge wall, which seemed to reach almost to heaven. "Nineveh!" gasped Little Worm, shivering in anticipation. *Now what should I do?* he wondered.

While Little Worm was still pondering the vista before him a lizard trotted jauntily up. Little Worm didn't like the looks of him at all, but Little Worm didn't know the Wonder Maker had sent the lizard along to give him a ride. "Hi, my name is Licky," the lizard said. "Hop up, little fellow," he invited, motioning for Little Worm to climb aboard. "Those tiny silk shoes will burn up in all this hot sand."

"Well . . . why . . . how did you know I would be here?" Little Worm asked, noticing the lizard had a bunch of orange, green, and red suckers in a small pouch hanging from his neck.

The lizard giggled and popped a fresh sucker in his mouth. His tiny tongue flicked at high speed on all sides of the candy. "Don't worry, worm! I get my orders from the top. You better come along now."

Little Worm still didn't like Licky's looks, but his feet were starting to burn. Hanging on tightly to his precious cocoon, Little Worm crawled onto Licky Lizard's back. Before he could get properly seated Little Worm found himself flying across the red hot desert at a tremendous "lick." He began to feel quite ill, then remembered that Grubby Grub had put some travel pills in the cocoon. Opening the door with great difficulty, he found the pills—slightly squished—and swallowed them down. After that he felt fine and was able to enjoy his unusual ride.

As suddenly as Licky Lizard had started he stopped, tumbling Little Worm and his cocoon right off his back. "There you are," he said cheerfully. "You'll be alright now." And with that he scampered away to catch some mangey mosquitoes who, themselves, were looking for a bite to eat.

Little Worm looked up and saw he was right in front of the city's huge gate. Moving out of the scorching sun, he found a crack at the foot of one of the gateposts and rested in the pleasant shade. He nearly jumped out of his skin when another worm suddenly appeared from around the corner. He looked Little Worm over from tip to tip, which didn't take very long! Little Worm had never seen a town worm before. One of his distant cousins lived in the city, but Little Worm had never met

him and had no idea what he was like. Town Worm peered at him most suspiciously and obviously wanted him to explain what he was doing there.

"Ah . . . ah . . . I'm Little Worm," he said at last. "I live by a pond—three ponds away—and I'm really not at all sure why I've come to Nineveh!" He felt very silly saying that and not a little timid. Town Worm looked so very clever. He didn't wear big horn-rimmed glasses like Book Worm, but as Little Worm looked into his eyes he saw small plastic discs—contact lenses! Book Worm had told him town worms were very far ahead of country worms in such matters. Town Worm did look extremely intelligent. He had a furrowed forehead, and big bags hung beneath his weak eyes. *Maybe those came from staying up late at night studying,* thought Little Worm, gazing intently at the bags. *If he is so smart, maybe he could read the instructions on the side of the cocoon.* "Can you read?" Little Worm asked him timidly.

"Can I read?" exclaimed Town Worm. "Of course I can read, *stupid*. All the worms in Nineveh can read! What sort of a country cousin are you to ask such a question?" Town Worm walked around Little Worm and noticed the cocoon. "What's this?" he asked. "It looks like a very expensive cocoon indeed. I've never seen one quite like it. Who gave it to you? Did you steal it?" he ended suspiciously.

"No, I did not!" replied Little Worm, forgetting his

fear and becoming angry. "The Wonder Maker spun it for me, and He has sent me here to do some work for Him."

"I don't believe you," Town Worm replied roughly. "Why ever would the Wonder Maker choose someone like you to do His work? Why you can't even read!"

"Maybe I can't read," answered Little Worm with sudden spirit, "but I do know how to treat strangers politely!"

Town Worm flushed. He did feel badly about his lack of hospitality. Little Worm looked tired and dusty, and he was so very, very small. He was right! This was no way to treat a stranger.

"Come along then," he muttered gruffly, and, lifting the cocoon on his back, he motioned for Little Worm to follow him. However, his legs were so much longer and stronger than his country cousin's, and he set off at such a rapid pace that it didn't take more than a moment or two before he quite disappeared from sight!

"Where—where did he go?" gasped Little Worm, looking this way and that. Just then Town Worm popped his head out of a crack in a gatepost up ahead and called impatiently, "Can't you keep up? You'll get squashed flat by a chariot wheel if you stay out there like that!"

Little Worm scurried into the crack and found himself in the hollowed-out hallway of Town Worm's home.

TOWN WORM

It was most interesting and not a bit like any of the country cottages he was used to back at the Pond. There was a huge can of termite spray on a shelf, an Encyclopedia Nivannica next to it, and a yashmak hanging on a hook on the wall. Little Worm had heard about yashmaks and knew they were scarf-like things used to cover your face. Seeing Little Worm looking at his yashmak Town Worm said, "I bought it from an eastern worm from Arabia last market day. I'll lend it to you if you'd like, when you go into town. Nineveh is full of red dust that gives you awful sinus trouble."

"Oh," said Little Worm, not wanting to ask what sinus trouble was.

"Just look at these bags under my eyes," continued Town Worm. "That's because the dust gets up my nose and it has to go somewhere!"

So that's what's in those bags, thought Little Worm. *It must be awful to live in such a dusty place.* The air was always so beautifully clear and clean back home by his beloved pond.

Town Worm led his new friend down a narrow corridor and into a comfortable living room where several other Town Worms were plopped in stuffed chairs smoking cigarettes, reading newspapers, and discussing politics. No one seemed to notice him, so he crawled to a dark corner and sat silently, eager to learn what he could.

"Nineveh will win, of course," a military-looking worm with a handlebar moustache said.

"But Israel's soldiers are fierce and fight to the death," replied another.

"That may be," argued a small red furry thing, busily combing the dust out of his whiskers. "But the fact remains they are no match for the Assyrians."

Little Worm realized they were talking about a war the fierce Ninevites were planning against Israel. *Oh dear,* he thought, *if these Ninevites attack the Wonder Maker's people, they will have to drive their big chariots right down the forest path past the Pond. Whatever will become of us?*

One of the worms suddenly noticed Little Worm sitting in the corner. "Who are you and where did you come from?" he asked suspiciously.

"I'm Little Worm," he answered in a little voice, "and I've come from a pond, three ponds away."

"That's a very long way to come," commented Wriggly Worm, struggling into some overalls. She picked up a broom and began sweeping up the fine red dust that had seeped in through the cracks in the gatepost and now covered the floor.

"He's a missionary," said Town Worm in a voice meant to impress the others. At that everybody stopped what they were doing and gathered around the visitor. Little Worm glowed. He felt so good being described in

TOWN WORM

such a way. Besides, it was quite dark in the room by now, so his little light had begun to show.

"Look, he's all lit up!" exclaimed Wriggly Worm excitedly.

"Missionaries always shine like that," said Worldly Worm pompously, wanting everyone to know he knew everything about everything.

"Oh no, we don't!" Little Worm assured him hastily. "We glow only when it's dark, or when we are joyfully doing the Wonder Maker's work."

"Well, what have you been sent to do?" demanded Worldly Worm.

Little Worm had hoped very hard they wouldn't ask that question. "I don't know," he answered in barely a whisper.

"You don't know?" the worms cried in unison. "Whoever heard of a missionary who didn't know what he's supposed to be doing!"

"Well, sometimes you don't know," Little Worm said defensively. "The Wonder Maker hasn't told me yet, and He must have His own good reasons. I have done all that I *do* know to do, and that's all He expects from any of us. He told me to come here and get instructions."

"Well, you can't stay here until you get them," said Town Worm briskly. "There's no room. I did have a spare bed, but those wretched termites ate it while I was out of town last week."

Little Worm's furry head drooped sadly. Wriggly Worm suddenly felt sorry for him, and wriggling near she tugged at his antenna and whispered that he should follow her. Little Worm obeyed, and after crawling through a narrow passageway and making their way past many nooks and crevices, the inching pair came finally into the strong sunlight in the midst of the bustling, hustling city of Nineveh.

Talk Time
1. Why did Town Worm have bags under his eyes?
2. Do you think the Worker believed in miracles? Why? Do you believe in miracles?
3. Who was with the Worker inside the fish? What can we learn from that?

Prayer time

Thank the Wonder Maker for being with us at all times, *EVEN* when we are being disobedient.

5
Holes

Little Worm had never seen anything like it. People were everywhere. Great iron chariots rumbled along the dusty streets, driven by cruel-faced men who whipped the sweating horses along at a terrible speed. Merchants bought and sold, cheating their customers as often as they could, while robbers stood waiting in the shadows, ready to steal goods from anyone.

Just for fun, some small vicious boys were cutting off a cat's tail with a sharp stone. Not far from them a girl with an ugly mean face gleefully stuck her finger in a baby's eye!

Shouting, screaming, and crying filled the air. And the red dust hung in clouds, decorating the trees with orange soot and stuffing up Little Worm's nose. *Oh dear me,* he thought, *I'll soon have bags under my eyes like Town Worm!*

Wriggly Worm pulled her wide-eyed companion along the wall of the city until they turned off into a side crack and entered the City of Worms. Little Worm noticed at once that it was market day.

"I have a stall here," said Wriggly Worm, leading him through a mass of maggots being prepared by merchants for resale to fishermen. Little Worm felt sorry for the maggots. He wasn't used to seeing grubs of any kind imprisoned and used cruelly by their own kind. Back at the Pond everyone was free to live as they chose. Trying to forget the little creatures' sad faces, Little Worm turned his attention back to his friend. "What do you sell in your stall?" he asked.

"Holes," replied Wiggly Worm.

"Holes?" gasped Little Worm.

"Yes, holes," she snapped. "I dig very nice holes, bring them to my store, and then sell most of them to Wealthy Worm, who has lots of ground to put them into. He rents them out."

"Oh," said Little Worm, staring at the rows and rows of simply beautiful holes displayed in Wriggly Worm's stall. Each had a unique shape and was cast in a different size. He saw one he would love to buy and take back for Silk Worm and himself, but scolded himself for thinking such thoughts. After all he probably would never see her again.

Wriggly Worm reached underneath her stall, pulled out some delicious flower stalks to chew on, and generously shared them with Little Worm. "If you will watch

my store today, I'll loan you one of my holes to live in while you are staying in Nineveh," she said.

Little Worm was delighted, but then he thought of something. "But where could I put it?" he asked. "I don't have any ground here." At the Pond finding a lot wouldn't have been a problem; the forest had plenty of room. But here in the city all the land belonged to someone already.

"Well, why don't you put wheels on it," suggested Wriggly Worm. "I just happen to have a pair of old roller skates here in a drawer. You can take the wheels off and fasten them under your hole. That way you can move around the city, park where you like for the night, and disappear inside your hole if trouble comes!"

Little Worm hugged Wriggly Worm thankfully and settled down to watch the store. He began to attach the wheels to a beautiful hole that Wriggly Worm had picked out for him.

Silently, and as always without warning, the Wonder Maker appeared; He laughed when He saw Little Worm working so hard. "Why, Little Worm," He said in the voice that sounded like a million waterfalls, "I think this is a good place for you to be! Selling holes is just the right sort of thing for a 'holy' worm like you!"

Little Worm laughed, too, and thanked the Wonder Maker for providing for him on his journey. "Have you come to tell me what I'm to do?" he asked, hopefully.

"I've come to tell you the *next* thing I want you to do," replied the Wonder Maker. "You don't need to know anything more than that at the present."

Little Worm was a bit disappointed. *When will the Wonder Maker tell me the reason for this great journey?* he wondered. *Why did it all have to be such a secret?*

"Trust Me, Little Worm," said the Wonder Maker, as if He could read his thoughts, which of course He could.

Sighing, Little Worm nodded. "All right, what is the *next* thing You want me to do?"

"I want you to pack the cocoon in the hole and wheel it to the marketplace by noon tomorrow. Wriggly Worm will tell you how to get there," said the Wonder Maker.

Little Worm promised he would do as he'd been told, and turning his attention to the job at hand, set about selling Wriggly Worm's holes.

At first trade was slow. There had been a recession in Nineveh, and worms were making do with their old holes, patching them up and painting over the cracks to save money. But there were some wealthy worms in Nineveh, and soon Little Worm was busy showing customers the different holes. A young couple came to look, and they were so rude that Little Worm felt a bit intimidated. Nothing was right with anything that Little Worm showed them. The lady worm was especially hard to please and kept poking holes in all of his sales arguments. She not only argued with Little Worm, she quarreled with her husband too, and Little Worm found himself standing between them while they both tried to hit each other over the head! Since he was in the middle, Little Worm got hit most of all and in the end sold them a hole at half price just to get rid of them.

As he wrapped up their package he noticed the couple grinning at each other. He had the nastiest suspicion that their fight had been a put-up job to make him sell the hole cheap! He felt quite cross about it, but handed over the parcel and bade them good-bye as politely as he could. *What different worms these are from the worms at home,* he thought. *Why, the whole of Nineveh seemed to be crooked or cross, from the top to the very bottom!*

Only a half-day's journey from Nineveh, the Worker awakened and found that the Wonder Maker had provided a lovely breakfast for him. It had been carried in by ravens and was served by sparrows. The man shook the sleep from his eyes and ate his fill. He was glad to see that the birds had brought him bread and fruit. If they had provided fish, he would've been sick on the spot! He decided he would never be able to eat fish again as long as he lived.

The Worker felt marvelous today. Not only was he

safely out of the Whale's stomach, he was strong again and ready to go to Nineveh. Something caught his eye in a nearby tree, and glancing up he noticed a letter fluttering in the branches. He climbed up to retrieve it and tore open the envelope eagerly. It was the Wonder Maker's message for the Assyrians: "Tell the people of Nineveh that unless they repent, their city will be overthrown within forty days."

Well, now, that was great news! The Worker was delighted with the Wonder Maker's message. He was sure there was no chance of the evil men of Nineveh even listening to him, much less stopping their evil ways. The Wonder Maker would destroy them after all, and then his beloved country of Israel would be safe. Chuckling with delight, he gathered his ragged robes around his waist, thanked the birds for his breakfast, and ran on his way rejoicing.

Soon he arrived at the great city gates. Nineveh was such a big city, it looked as if it would take three whole days just to walk all the way around it. What a lot of work the Wonder Maker had given him to do. Most of the villages in Israel were small, and it was quite easy to gather all the people together to hear his sermons. In Nineveh he would have to find a central place and try to attract a crowd. Perhaps he would have to hold many meetings before everybody had heard the Wonder Maker's message.

And just how am I to get the people to listen to me? he wondered. In Israel he was well known. People respected him and recognized him as a prophet from the clothing that he wore. Here in this strange land he feared he would not be noticed at all. But he needn't have worried! As soon as he began to walk through the city shouting out his message, the Ninevites began to come from every side, surrounding him and calling to others to come and hear what he had to say. *Why are they all staring at me?* the Worker thought, not a little frightened.

The people crowded against him, but they were friendly. Some of them touched his skin and others pointed to his hair. *Whatever is the matter with me?* puzzled the Worker. *Is it my strange clothes? Is it because I'm from Israel?*

He had no way of knowing how he now looked. During his dreadful ordeal in the fish's stomach the Worker had continually been sprayed with acids. Because of this his hair and skin had been bleached the weirdest white imaginable. Even his eyebrows and beard were a translucent, silvery color. No one in Nineveh had ever seen such a strange-looking man. In the eyes of the superstitious Assyrians he seemed like some god who had come to visit from another world.

Instinctively, the Worker realized the Ninevites were thinking this, although he had no idea why, and he interrupted their excited chatter to assure them that he was not a god but just a man. He told them that he served the Wonder Maker, who had kept him alive inside a big fish at the bottom of the ocean so that he could come and tell them his message. To the Worker's amazement the people believed him. The throng eagerly urged him to tell them every word of God's message to them. The Worker could not believe his ears, but unknown to him, in the Wonder Maker's marvelous plan, the sailors from Joppa had been playing a key role in aiding his mission in Nineveh.

After surviving the big storm, the sailors who had been on the Worker's ship steered it back to the quay in Joppa and tumbled ashore. They called the people standing around the little fishing stores to gather and hear their amazing story. Everybody was surprised to see the sailors back so soon, because the ship was usually gone for days at a time. Only that morning the people of the port city had waved the sailors off, wishing them well and praying that the gods would grant them safety.

When the storm had sprung up everyone had been surprised. It had not been the usual sort of storm that first appeared far out to sea and gave them plenty of warning. It had erupted from "nowhere" and died away just as quickly. The wives and the children of the sailors had been worried about their men.

The sailors told the huge crowd their tale. When the storm struck, they had lightened their craft by throwing all the cargo over the side. Without their fishing tackle, there had been no point in continuing their journey, so they had returned.

The most amazing part of their story was the bit about the man who had been running away from his God. The sailors explained how he had been asleep at the bottom of the boat until their captain had waked him up and urged him to pray to his God to stop the storm.

"The man told us the storm was raging because his God was angry with him for running away, and that the only way to stop it was to pick him up and throw him overboard!" said a young, bearded sailor excitedly. "We tried to bring the ship around, but we couldn't. There was nothing left for us to do but pray to the man's God, to ask Him to forgive us. So we did, and then we cast the man into the sea."

The listening crowd gasped in horror. "What happened then?" a little boy cried out.

"The storm stopped all at once!" an older sailor replied. "We fell to our knees and told the man's God we would fear and serve Him forever. Why, what god of our fathers has even been known to make the sea stop its raging?"

"What's more," another sailor added, "we saw a huge sea monster to starboard, following the man down into the depths and. . . ."

"Oh no, oh no," murmured the people, "what a death, what a death!" A shudder ran through the crowd and there was a long silence. All wondered what awful thing the man had done to come to such a dreadful end.

After the crowd broke up, the sailors discussed what to do next. They would have to start all over again since they had no wares to sell at Tarshish. They decided to go to Nineveh and buy the goods they needed. And so they sailed to that great city, telling the merchants there why they had come, repeating again the whole exciting tale of the Wonder Maker's prophet from Israel and how he had most assuredly perished in the jaws of the sea monster.

It was, therefore, no wonder that later the people of Nineveh listened to the Worker. As soon as they saw his bleached skin and listened to his story and heard his strange message, they knew exactly who he was—and they believed! After all, a God who could bring His prophet back from a fish's stomach at the bottom of the sea would have no trouble at all overthrowing their city. They listened to the strange man very carefully.

And so the Worker found the people of Nineveh willing to accept his awesome message. He didn't understand why they paid him heed, and he certainly wasn't pleased about it, but he was obedient and went on his way among the people, crying out—"Forty days, and Nineveh will be overthrown."

One of those who heard the Worker was the captain of the King's chariot fleet. Calling a runner aside, he whispered in his ear: "Go quickly and tell the King all that you have seen and heard." The slave nodded his head and vanished on flying feet.

Talk Time

1. What sort of people lived in Nineveh?
2. Why do you think the people listened to Jonah?
3. Why do you think the Wonder Maker cared for the people of Nineveh when they were so wicked?

Prayer Time

Pray for people who have never had a chance to hear about the Wonder Maker.
Pray for the missionaries that tell them.

6
The Wicked King

The King was in his counting house counting all his money. He was in a hurry because some new slaves had been captured, and he needed to go and inspect them. He would have to decide which of them should live and which of them should die. The small boys and girls and some of the strong young men would be saved, but the old and sick and many of the women he would have killed. He was a cruel and terrible king and had no pity for the poor captured creatures who cried out for mercy.

One of his military commanders entered the room with an evil smirk upon his face. "King, sire," he said, "your chief chariot-makers have devised a dreadful new invention for your war machines. They would like you to come and see it."

Now the King was in a quandary. He needed to see the new slaves; he hadn't finished counting his money; and he wanted to find out what terrible weapon of torture his men had devised. In the end his curiosity won out, and he went with the commander of his troops.

Marching through the dusty, noisy, rough street, the King, along with his commander and some soldiers, reached the marketplace where a huge throng of people was gathered around an iron chariot. Using metal prongs and whips, the King's soldiers pushed the rude, noisy people aside. "Make way for the King," snarled the commander.

As the King examined the chariot he began to laugh—a tormented, terrible sound that began like a rumble of thunder and ended like the vicious barking of a mad dog. He saw at once what had been done. Sharp spikes protruded from each of the chariot wheels. They had been finely filed at one edge so that they were razor sharp. They looked like long vicious saws.

In his mind the King could picture his soldiers driving the chariot among his enemies, running the machine into defenseless crowds of people. He knew exactly what would happen, and he cackled with evil glee at the very thought of it. The sharp knives would slice his foes into thin ribbons before his men even stepped down from their chariots to fight. "Take care so you don't kill everyone in the next battle," he said to them in jest. "Save a few slaves for me, won't you!"

The soldiers began talking among themselves of torture, killing, and dreadful sorrows, for these were dark and cruel days and human flesh was cheap.

Across the city, Little Worm had packed up his goods and chattels, loaded his precious cocoon into his hole on wheels, and said thank you and good-bye to Wriggly Worm. He pushed his portable home along the red dusty street toward the marketplace. His little heart was pounding. *What will I find in the market square?* he wondered. The Wonder Maker had simply told him to go there without any explanation.

Little Worm thought about doing things without knowing why. To know the beginning was one thing, but not to know the end was another! If from the first the Wonder Maker had allowed him to know what lay ahead, he was sure he would not have been so worried. He even might have been more obedient along the way!

He knew the Wonder Maker could see the end from the beginning; in fact, Book Worm had told him once that one of the Wonder Maker's special names was "The Beginning and the End." That sounded like a very strange name for somebody, except it told you something about Him. It told you He had been there at the beginning and that He would be there at the end. And He would be there all the way in between too!

The very idea of this made Little Worm glow all over with sweet pleasure. As long as the Wonder Maker was there all the time, Little Worm decided that he really didn't mind being left in the dark. *It will be alright,* he reassured himself. *Yes, it will be alright. After all, obedience is doing what you are told without having to know why,* Little Worm concluded.

Little Worm suddenly realized he had arrived at the marketplace. His ideas had so absorbed him that he had not noticed the thickening of the crowd. People were crushed against people, carts against carts. Bundles of calico, stacks of clay pots, baskets of beans and wheat, crates of desert sandals, and piles of precious firewood were all being hauled to market. But something else was happening; Little Worm could hear shouts ahead, something about the King coming.

Pushing his hole along quickly (it ran very smoothly on the little wheels) he nearly collided with Town Worm, who was climbing up the side of a brick, straining his neck to get a better view of the commotion. "Hello," he said to Little Worm. "What are you doing here?"

Before Little Worm had time to answer, Town Worm pointed a shaky antenna at a huge man dressed in very royallooking robes. The man was standing beside the weirdest looking chariot Little Worm had ever seen. "That's the King," Town Worm informed his country cousin in an awed whisper.

Little Worm had never seen a king before. The man certainly looked very "kingly," dressed in splendid rich robes. But Little Worm didn't like the King's face very much. The mouth was hard, the eyes cold, and it looked as though he never smiled. The King's gaze was riveted to the chariot. Little Worm had only seen chariots once before—when Wriggly Worm led him to the heart of Nineveh. But his Aunt Ethel back at the Pond had a picture book that had been one of Little Worm's favorites. All sorts of different chariots were pictured in it, but this one here in Nineveh's market square didn't look like any in Aunt Ethel's book! There was something particularly ugly and somehow sinister about it.

"Just look at all those knife things sticking out of the wheels," hissed Town Worm. "When the wheels go round, the knives will cut people to pieces!"

The King leaned over to speak to the soldier sitting in the chariot. Without any warning, the man raised his whip and struck the horses that were harnessed to the chariot. The wheels of the iron machine spun and the knives flashed in the strong sunlight, slicing into the crowd, splattering bloody bits of people onto the ground! The chariot stopped amid the cries of the dying. Screams from their family and friends rang from the crowd. Blood was everywhere.

Little Worm gazed in horror at the awful sight. Looking to his right, he was shocked to see that Town Worm had been buried under a pile of blood-splattered dust, but even as Little Worm looked the mound moved. Dazed and shaken, Town Worm shook his head, staggered to his feet, and shouted, "Look out," then scurried down a convenient crack into Worm Land. Glancing upward Little Worm shuddered. The huge sole of a boot was moving toward him in the sky right above his head. Almost paralyzed with fright, he remembered his hole. Crawling faster than he ever had in his entire life, he clambered into it and found himself safe and sound as the awful boot scrunched overhead.

Shivering with shock, Little Worm began to cry. He wanted to forget the terrible things he had just witnessed. How could the King be so horribly evil? His own people had been killed just so he could see how the new chariot worked! Through the walls of his hole Little Worm could still hear the laughter of the cruel King as he walked callously away from the dead people, quite untouched at all the suffering he had caused. Having had his fun, he was going back to count his money and inspect the batch of wretched slaves.

Little Worm thought about the Worker. No wonder he ran away when he had been told to go to Nineveh. He must have known how bad the people were and realized they would never listen to his message from the Wonder Maker.

Feeling very, very lonely, Little Worm reached inside the cocoon for the wedding picture of his mother and father. The sight of those dear fuzzy faces made him cry. He wished he had never left his beloved Pond and the security of his home to serve the Wonder Maker. He hadn't known that obedience could be so frightening and dangerous. He had believed that the Wonder Maker would protect him, if he did the Wonder Maker's will. Now Little Worm wasn't so sure—he had nearly been killed by that big boot only a minute ago! His furry body shaking with fright, Little Worm cried and cried and cried, his tears pattering down the walls of the hole, collecting at the bottom. How sorry he felt for himself.

Then the Voice that sounded like a million waterfalls interrupted Little Worm's pity party, and he stopped crying so he could listen. *Perhaps He has come to tell me I can go home,* Little Worm thought. *Maybe He just wanted to see if I would obey Him and now He's come to send me back to the Pond!*

But the Wonder Maker was not saying anything like that to Little Worm. As Little Worm gazed into the hole that had somehow become a fathomless depth, he saw the eternal Face, which bore the saddest eternal look. The eternal hands were cupped around Little Worm's tears, guiding them gently into an eternal bottle. The Wonder Maker's voice could be heard, saying distinctly, "One, two, three, four."

"Why, why—He's counting my tears!" stammered Little Worm incredulously. Beyond the eternal Face stood a great and shiny being, an angel. The beautiful creature held a quill pen and in front of him lay an eternal book. After the Wonder Maker counted each of

Little Worm's tears a mark was carefully recorded on a clean page. Then Little Worm remembered a sermon he had heard in Israel a few months ago—the time when Book Worm had visited the Pond on a holy day to read the Wonder Maker's Psalms. One verse in a Psalm had really puzzled him, but he had been too little and shy to ask what it meant. He remembered the words, "Put my tears into your bottle—Are they not in your book?" Now, at last he understood. Little Worm's little heart seemed to explode in pure joy, and the inside of his hole shimmered with the glow of his whole soul as he worshiped the Wonder Maker and thanked Him for His eternal care.

When he opened his eyes after his prayer of thanksgiving, the eternal Face and the angel had disappeared. Little Worm picked up the photo of his mother and father and, as he slid it carefully back inside the cocoon, he noticed something different about the photograph. He gasped! His parents were smiling at him in the same strange way they had smiled at him the day he had left the Pond. He was quite sure they had not been smiling that way in the picture before. Happily, he put the precious picture safely away.

Little Worm closed the door of his cocoon, climbed gingerly up the inside of his hole, and peeped over the top. One look caused him to tumble right down again. He could hardly believe his eyes. In the middle of the marketplace, right where the King had examined the chariot, stood the strangest man he had ever seen. His hair was solid white and his skin was a silvery color. His clothes were tattered and his sandals worn. Somehow, his face looked familiar.

While the man gathered a crowd around him, some children, looking for something to steal, rummaged through the pockets of the dead people whose bodies still littered the city square. Dogs nosed the corpses, and occasionally someone would kick them away. Other people, ignoring the misery and bloodshed, screamed the prices of their wares from market stalls. But once the strange-looking man began to preach, the crowd grew quiet and gathered around him. "Yet forty days, and Nineveh shall be overthrown," he cried in his prophet's voice.

"It's him!" shouted Little Worm. "It's him! It's him! It's the Wonder Maker's Worker! He's come, oh, he's come! He must have changed his mind and decided to do the Wonder Maker's will after all."

Little Worm was so excited he popped right out of the top of his hole. People were listening to every word the Worker had to say. Little Worm scanned the crowd with amazement. *They'll kill him, for sure,* he worried. *Who will believe such a prophet of doom?* He knew the people had just seen the terrible war chariot, and they believed their army was stronger than any other army in the world. They would never believe the Wonder Maker's message.

Of course Little Worm had not heard about the Worker's ordeal. Nor did he know about the sailors. He hadn't heard their excited reports of how the Wonder Maker's Worker from Israel had been killed by a big fish . . . so he couldn't understand why the people were paying such close attention. They thought the Worker had come back from the dead! No wonder they believed him!

By this time an absolute quietness had fallen upon the crowd. All eyes were upon the Worker. Suddenly, there came sounds of a loud commotion at the opposite side of the square. Harsh noises filled the air as the King's captain and his men ran into the space in front of the Worker. Little Worm paled—now it would all be over. The Worker would be captured, tortured, and killed!

"Make way for the King!" shouted the King's captain, and with a flurry and scurry people scampered out of the way. There, approaching the brave Worker and the crowd of people who had been listening to his every word, strode the King of Assyria, the ruler of Nineveh himself!

Talk Time

1. How many words can you think of to describe the wicked king?
2. How many words can you think of to describe the Worker as he told the people about the Wonder Maker?
3. Why is it hard to do what we are told without knowing why?

Prayer Time

Pray for parents that they may be fair and loving.

7
Really, Really, *Really* Sorry

Perched on top of his little hole Little Worm had a clear view of the town square. His heart was beating very fast. He wondered what the King might do to the Worker. Little Worm didn't know if he liked the Worker but, then, he didn't really know him very well. The only other time he had seen him was that day in the forest when the Worker had run down the path with that sad, strange look upon his face. But today Little Worm was certainly glad to see him, for here was someone standing very close to him who also had been sent to Nineveh to do the Wonder Maker's work. They had something very important in common: they both loved and served the Wonder Maker.

The thought of this excited Little Worm, and hastily scrambling into his hole, he fished out Grumpy Grub's lovely red bandanna. Reappearing, he waved the kerchief furiously over his head, trying to attract the Worker's attention. He wanted to welcome him and to let him know that there was at least one on his side in the strange, silent crowd that surrounded him.

When the King appeared in the town square, everyone fell back a step or two. The dead people still lay in the street, and some in the crowd tripped over the bodies as they pushed each other back out of the way. The people were afraid the King might have some other little trick to play on them. But they needn't have worried. The King walked up to the Worker and shouted in a loud voice, "Tell us your story, Prophet; we are listening."

The Worker, who now stood on the steps of the tallest building in the marketplace, towered above the King. *What an impressive and frightening figure he is,* thought Little Worm. The Worker's eyes flashed with anger, and his right arm was pointed toward heaven. "The Wonder Maker has told me to come here," he cried out. "He has sent me to tell you to be really, really, *really* sorry, or within forty days He will overthrow your great city of Nineveh."

Little Worm could hardly believe that everyone, including the mighty King, was listening intently to the Worker's words. Then the King walked up to the Prophet and rubbed his bleached skin and fingered his white hair. "Yes," he said, "you are truly the man from Israel who the sailors from Joppa told us about."

The Worker went on to tell the people that he had not wanted to come and give them the Wonder Maker's message, and so he had run away. But the Wonder Maker had sent a huge sea monster to bring him to Nineveh.

"They believe him, they believe him!" gasped Little Worm incredulously, gazing around the circle of frightened faces.

The Worker ended his speech, and pandemonium broke loose. Standing in the midst of that huge throng, the King of Nineveh did the strangest thing. In front of everyone he stripped himself of his royal robes and called for his servants to bring forth some sackcloth, which he draped over his shoulders. People all around followed suit, stripping off their garments, some of them ripping their cloaks to shreds. Next some men dashed around the market square, moving the cooking pots filled with hot soup and scattering the hot coals underneath the vessels. They dug their hands into the ashes and threw the hot dust into the air, crying out to the Wonder Maker for mercy.

Meanwhile, the King had collected some of the hot ashes and had mixed them with the thick, red dirt that lay everywhere—arranging it all in one big heap. *Goodness me,* thought Little Worm, aghast, *I think he's going to sit in those ashes!* Sure enough he was—and sure enough he did, right in the middle of the pile, to be exact!

In the midst of this excitement Town Worm ap-

peared again. After hearing the commotion overhead, his curiosity had bested him, and he had surfaced to see what was going on.

"Just look at the King sitting in the ashes," Little Worm said excitedly to him. "It can't be very comfortable!"

"It's not supposed to be comfortable, silly," Town Worm snapped. "He's trying to show the Wonder Maker he's really, really, *really* sorry."

The King shouted for a "cryer" to come forth from among his men. Little Worm could hardly see an inch in front of his face by this time—so much dust and ashes had been tossed into the air by the frenzied men. "Put your bandanna on," urged Town Worm, showing him how to tie it tightly over his nose and mouth.

Town Worm had pulled his yashmak over his face, and Little Worm had to smile . . . his friend looked quite funny. But the bright red bandanna did help a lot, and Little Worm now could watch the proceedings without coughing and sneezing. He invited Town Worm to climb beside him atop the hole, for a better view.

The Cryer now stood before the King who was telling him the message he wanted carried throughout the Royal Realm. Turning away from his majesty, who was jumping about a bit on his heap of hot ashes, the Cryer began to cry: "Hear ye, hear ye, what the King has decreed."

"What's 'decreed'?" asked Little Worm in a muffled voice through his red bandanna.

"Decided," Town Worm answered, impatiently.

"Let neither man nor beast, herd nor flock, taste anything. Do not let them eat, or drink water," the Cryer shouted. "But let man and beast be covered with sackcloth and cry mightily to the Wonder Maker. Yea, let everyone turn from his evil way and from the violence that is in his hands." After this the Cryer ran off to another neighborhood in Nineveh.

Everyone in the city square was shouting at everyone else, urging each other to do what the King had commanded. A royal wail arose from the royal heap of ashes. "Who can tell if God will turn away from His fierce anger and not destroy us?" cried the King.

"He *is* sorry," said Little Worm to Town Worm. "He's really, really, *really* sorry!"

"It's alright *saying* you're sorry," retorted Town Worm. "That's easy to do. But the Wonder Maker will want to see if he really, really, really *means* it! In the next few days He will be watching what the King *does*, not just listening to what he *says*!"

Dragging Little Worm inside the hole with him, Town Worm suggested that they stay out of harm's way until the evening after everyone had gone home. And so it was. When they eventually popped out of Little Worm's hole again, the Worker had gone on his way, and the King and all the people had returned to their homes. Dust still hung heavily in the air, and Little Worm was very thirsty. Climbing out onto the street, Little Worm and Town Worm pushed the hole on wheels into the crack in the sidewalk and back to Town Worm's house.

The next few days were the most exciting of Little Worm's life. Everywhere he went he saw evidence that the people of Nineveh were really, really, *really* sorry for their evil ways. The first day Little Worm saw the girl with the ugly face who had so cruelly hurt the poor baby. She had found the little one after hours of searching and was busy bathing the child's red and swollen eye with a piece of clean cloth. The girl's lips were swollen with thirst, but she wanted to show the Wonder Maker that she was really, really, *really* sorry. So instead of drinking the precious water she carried, she used it to cleanse the baby's wound.

Little Worm squirmed past the stalls in the market square. There was the most terrible commotion because dozens of thieves were trying to give back the things that they had stolen from each other. Everywhere, people swept up heaps of dust and ashes and sat down in them. Then they pulled their torn robes or pieces of dirty sackcloth over their heads and pleaded with the Wonder Maker for mercy.

The King called his servants and ordered them to

visit the relatives of the poor people who had been killed by the sharp chariot knives. Though he couldn't bring the dead people back to life (only the Wonder Maker can do that), he sent money and gifts from his own treasury and appointed the older members of their families nobles in his land.

"Come on!" Town Worm excitedly called to Little Worm. "Let's go inside and see what's happening." Little Worm followed his friend into Worm Land. The Worms knew that the destruction of Nineveh would mean their end as well, so they wanted to show the Wonder Maker that they were really, really, *really* sorry too.

Back inside the underground city Little Worm couldn't believe his eyes. As the two entered they were very nearly bowled over by a mass of maggots squirming and jumping in joy. They were chattering excitedly, because Wiley Worm, who had been intending to sell the maggots for fishing bait, had set them free!

Little Worm found Wiley Worm sitting in a big pile of dust and ashes, rocking himself to and fro and singing a sad, sad, sorry song he had made up all by himself. But what really pleased Little Worm the most was meeting Worldly Worm and Wealthy Worm wheeling a huge wheelbarrow, piled high with all the money Wealthy Worm had made from charging too much rent for his holes. On top of the money was most of the fine furniture from Wealthy Worm's mansion. The two rich worms were stopping at every Weak Worm's house to leave gifts. Little Worm barely recognized the two important creatures, because worms look awfully weird when dressed in sackcloth and sprinkled with ashes!

Town Worm had disappeared, and it was quite a long time before he showed up again, skidding to a stop right in front of Little Worm, a parcel wrapped in brown paper tucked underneath one of his legs. Little Worm noticed Town Worm's face was very red. He could tell it was red, even though a little pile of dust, perched in the middle of a bald spot on his head, was shedding white ashes all over him.

"Here," Town Worm said, pushing the parcel into Little Worm's arms.

"What is it?" asked Little Worm, surprised. "Open it—go on—open it," Town Worm urged, not answering the question and looking awkward and embarrassed. Little Worm unwrapped the parcel very carefully indeed. Inside were two pairs of blue silk running shoes! For a moment Little Worm was confused. *Why is Town Worm giving me more running shoes when he knows I have some already?* he thought. As Town Worm stood there speechless, shuffling from one foot to the other, Little Worm realized that these were *his* shoes and that Town Worm had stolen them from him.

"But when . . . when did you take them?" Little Worm asked in astonishment.

"When we were in the hole together at the marketplace," Town Worm replied, looking very guilty. "While you were watching the Worker preach his message, I reached inside the cocoon and took them! I had never seen anything so beautiful in my life."

"That's alright," Little Worm said kindly. "I'm glad you brought them back, though. A *very* special friend made them for me, and I would have hated to lose them. The Wonder Maker will be pleased to know what you have done." Town Worm smiled gratefully, turned on his tail, and scurried away.

As soon as Wriggly Worm saw that Little Worm was alone again, she grabbed his antenna and told him to hop into the hole. "I want to push you outside the city gates to see something amazing!" she said.

"All right," Little Worm answered, wondering if anything could be as amazing as the sight of all of Worm Land showing the Wonder Maker how really, really, *really* sorry they were.

Wriggly Worm pushed the hole along until they arrived right in the middle of a scrubby pasture outside the city gates. "You can come out now," she called to Little Worm, popping her head into the top of the hole.

Little Worm gazed around in awe. Sweaty, hot cows, sheep, and goats stood around miserably, weighted down heavily with layers and layers of sackcloth. They had been sprinkled with ashes, too, and their tongues were lolling from their mouths as they panted for water. It was so hot and they were very, very hungry, as well as parched with thirst. But not one of them lowered a head to feed or to drink. The animals wanted to have a part in showing the Wonder Maker that they were really, really, *really* sorry, too.

Horses neighed soft "sorrys" for all the times they had proudly drawn the terrible chariots of war. Goats bleated "sorry" for all the butting they had done, and cows blew their horns in a symphony of sadness. The city of Nineveh had truly repented.

Little Worm was beside himself with joy. As dusk fell on the great land full of dusty, parched people and animals, Little Worm knew that all from king and noble, to man and beast—even to the weeniest, weeny worm—were busy being really, really, *really* sorry for their sins.

"You have to *show* the Wonder Maker you're sorry, you see," Little Worm explained to Wriggly Worm. "You have to stop doing what you *have* been doing and start doing what you *should have* been doing all along. It's no good just being sorry because you've been caught, either; you've got to be so sorry *inside* that you start doing things *outside* to show you really mean it!"

In heaven the Wonder Maker looked down and saw it all, and the voice like the million waterfalls spoke: "I see your works and that you have turned from your evil ways and have truly changed your minds about your sin. Therefore, I shall show you mercy and change My mind about the evil I was going to bring upon you."

Hearing the Wonder Maker's words made Little Worm think of the Worker. It was a bit odd that he had vanished from the city square after preaching his sermon. Just as Little Worm thought about this the Wonder Maker appeared at his side. Wriggly Worm was so frightened, she tied herself into a knot, and Little Worm had to untie her and tell her not to be afraid. After she was unkinked, Little Worm took Wriggly Worm by the hand, introduced her to the Wonder Maker, and explained to Him how kind she had been when Little Worm had arrived in the city as a total stranger. The Wonder Maker smiled His smile at her, which caused Wriggly Worm to nearly melt away with happiness! She had never dreamed she would meet the Wonder Maker face to face.

"Thank you, Wriggly Worm," said the Wonder Maker. "You have given Little Worm a cup of cold water and a few of your own precious flower stalks for My sake, and I want you to know you shall in no way lose your reward!" Having said this He placed a letter in Wriggly Worm's hands, asked her to read it to Little Worm, and then was gone.

Wriggly Worm gazed at the letter in awe. The next episode of the Great Adventure was at hand!

Talk Time

1. What does the word "repent" mean?
2. How did the Ninevites show the Wonder Maker they were really sorry?
3. How did Town Worm show Little Worm he was sorry?

Prayer Time

Think of one thing you need to say you are sorry for as you pray; then say you are sorry to the person.

8
Early Bird

With trembling hands, Wriggly Worm opened the Wonder Maker's letter. *What will the message say?* Little Worm wondered. Wriggly Worm read the note aloud: "Go out of the city by the far gate, and then you shall be told what I want you to do."

"Oh dear," cried Little Worm, "He still hasn't told me what it is all about! One more step in the dark!"

"But you look so pretty when you step in the dark and do what the Wonder Maker tells you to do," Wriggly Worm encouraged him. "You glow all over."

Leaving the animals outside the city gates, Little Worm invited Wriggly Worm to ride inside the hole this time while he pushed it back to the City of Worms. Once they arrived Little Worm told everyone about the Wonder Maker's letter with the new travel instructions, and then he said good-bye. Wriggly Worm offered to go with him to the city limits. Little Worm thanked her and told her he would give her the hole back then, as he didn't think he would be needing it anymore. At the gates Wriggly Worm helped load the precious cocoon onto Little Worm's back and sent him on his way.

It was awfully hot. The sand burned Little Worm's feet, and he was forced to stop and put on Silk Worm's running shoes. He tried not to think about how hot and sweaty he felt and thought instead about all the people in Nineveh who had told the Wonder Maker they were sorry. That made him feel really good inside.

Suddenly, after rounding a big cactus, he came face to face—or rather face to foot—with the Worker. The man stood quite still in the desert, with his hands on his hips, looking very angry indeed. Little Worm realized that the man hadn't seen him, for his eyes were turned toward heaven and he was talking with the Wonder Maker. Little Worm listened to the conversation in amazement. The Worker was in a terrible temper. He was telling the Wonder Maker he was very upset that the Ninevites had repented.

Why ever would he be angry about that? puzzled Little Worm.

"I knew You would forgive them!" the Worker said, working himself into a rage. "That's why I didn't want to come here in the first place; that's why I ran away to Tarshish! You are far too kind and gracious, patient and loving. Those wicked people deserve to be punished for all the cruel, murderous things they have done!"

Then the voice like a million waterfalls spoke from the sky: "They may have done evil things, but what difference is there between them and you? Is it right for you to be angry?"

Now Little Worm understood—the Wonder Maker wanted the Worker to be really, really, *really* sorry too.

"All evil is evil," the Wonder Maker continued. "People kill because they get angry. Your heart needs changing too!" As soon as the Worker heard this heavenly rebuke, he turned furiously on his heels and stamped off into the desert.

Oh dear, thought Little Worm. *How upsetting this all is.* He thought how nice it would have been if the Worker had stayed in the city, now that the King, his nobles, and the people were really, really, *really* sorry. The Worker could have been such a help, teaching them more about the Wonder Maker and His ways. After all if the people had repented so readily, surely they would want to learn how to serve the Wonder Maker forever! But even as he thought about it, Little Worm knew it would never happen unless the Wonder Maker could change His servant's angry heart.

The sun beat down upon Little Worm's head. It felt as if he had stuck his head in an oven. He paused to take a nap under a scrub bush, and there he slept soundly until dawn the next day.

Rising refreshed hours later, Little Worm experienced a growing excitement. He felt that this day he would learn at last what the Wonder Maker wanted him to do. Uncurling himself from the stalk he had used as a bed, he peeped out from under the bush. Suddenly he felt a soft kiss upon his little cheek. Shocked, he glanced around, but no one was in sight. The same thing had happened to him before, and he struggled to recall where and when. And then he remembered! "Is that you, Wooey Wind?" he shouted excitedly.

"Who, ho-o, yo-o-o-o-o-o-o," chuckled the Wind. Little Worm could hardly speak, he was so happy. He had often wondered if he would ever again see anyone from back at the Pond. Even though he had only met the Wind that one time on the forest path, he seemed like an old friend. The problem was that Wooey Wind reminded him *too* much of home.

"Oh, do I have a lot to tell you," Little Worm squeaked in glee. "Can you stay for breakfast?" he asked hopefully.

"Surely, I ca-a-a-a-n," moaned the Wind, caressing his breezy stomach. "I haven't eaten for a-a-a-a-ges! The Wonder Maker sent me here from my ho-o-o-o-me in the East, and that's an aw-w-w-w-w-w-fully long way away."

Little Worm hurriedly collected sticks for a fire. The Wind helped by blowing up some branches from a dead desert tree, and soon the pair had quite a pile.

Rubbing two sticks together, Little Worm started a flame. Then the Wind blew the sparks softly into warm, glowing coals. Little Worm gathered a panful of his favorite food—pollen from a flowering desert shrub—and started to fry the delicate dust over the flames in the juice of cactus leaves.

As they ate their breakfast Little Worm told the Wind the story of the mass repentance at Nineveh. With each exciting stage of the story the Wind gave a gentle wh-h-h-h-h-h-h-h-h-h-h-istle, thoroughly enjoying the saga. "Well, Little Worm," he said at last when the tale was finished, "you've certainly se-e-e-e-e-n a lot of life since you left your mother and father, Grubby, Greedy, and Grumpy Grub ba-a-a-a-a-ck at the Pond!"

"Why are you here?" inquired Little Worm.

"I've come to beat upon the Wor-r-r-r-ker's head," the Wind answered, winding himself up into a brisk breeze at the very thought of it!

"Beat upon the Worker's head?" cried Little Worm. "Whatever for?"

The Wind chuckled, "To give him a headache." he answered. "Maybe if we get him feeling sor-r-r-r-r-ry enough for himself, he will stop being ang-r-r-r-y with other people!" With that the Wind flew around in circles stirring up the sand in a whirlwind and blowing particles all over the place.

"Don't do that!" Little Worm cried, shielding his

eyes. But even before the words left his mouth, the Wind rushed off toward a large hill on the east side of Nineveh.

Little Worm put out the fire by scattering the hot sticks. Since the Wonder Maker had not told him what to do next, he decided he might as well follow the Wind while he waited. He was curious to see if having sand blown in his face would make any change in the Worker's hard heart.

Meanwhile, the Worker was making himself a booth on the side of the hill. He knew that without some shady place he would die in the fierce heat. Not that he cared much at that moment whether he lived or whether he died. He was so angry he felt terrible. Temper takes away your appetite and ties your stomach into knots, and so he wasn't hungry—even though he hadn't had a meal for days. He wondered if the Wonder Maker would take away his life if he asked Him to. He felt so miserable he wanted to die.

Then he had another thought. Maybe, if he sat in his little booth long enough, the people who lived in Nineveh would stop being really, really, really sorry and start hurting and killing each other again. Then the Wonder Maker would have to judge them. *Yes,* thought the Worker, *that's what I'll do—just sit here and see what will become of the city!*

All that day he watched the red, dusty city, hoping

to see the fire of judgment fall upon Nineveh. Late that night, tired beyond measure, he fell into a fitful sleep.

Buried deep in the soil, just beside the booth the Worker had built to shield himself from the sun, lay the seed of a weed. It was a strange seed. The other seeds that lay near it had never seen one quite like it before. But then they did not know that the Wonder Maker had specially prepared the seed for this time.

"Grow, weed, grow," whispered the Wonder Maker, touching it with His eternal hand, changing its nature. The weed pushed from its skin and began to twist and turn its way up, up, up through the sandy desert soil. "Go to Nineveh," the Wonder Maker commanded it softly.

"Look at that weird weed!" shouted one little sleepy seed to the next. "Have you ever seen one grow so quickly?"

No one had ever seen such a thing, of course. But then no one had ever seen the Wonder Maker make the seed of a weed grow up in just a night before. Weeds weren't even supposed to grow in the dark.

"Will you look at that," exclaimed one of the Warm Worms who lived in the hot sand. As the Weird Weed pushed its mysterious way up through the sandy soil, Warm Worm rushed home. He wanted his warm wife to see the strange sight and brought her back quickly.

Winding and twining, the Weird Weed stretched upward until it broke through the surface of the sand. While a squirmy crowd of Warm Worms watched, the Weird Weed continued to expand, plaiting itself together, growing richer and greener by the minute. All night the weed grew, until in the end it towered above the desert, ready to cast a great shadow of cool darkness across the Worker when the sun shone again.

"Why," said Warm Worm in a warm voice of great awe, "however did that happen?"

"All in a night, too," whispered his warm wife. With that they burrowed down into the desert soil again, eager to tell their warm wee ones the amazing story.

Dawn lit the sky, and the desert sand came alive with desert life. Early Bird arrived early. He had flown throughout the night, searching for some rare eastern food to take home for a special celebration. After his last venture near Nineveh, he had decided never to return. But his memory of the sharp, jagged stone a wicked soldier had thrown at him had faded; besides, this time he would avoid the city and look for food in the wide open spaces. Now with the sun about to rise, he knew he must hurry or he would have trouble getting back to the cool forest glade.

Seeing nothing that looked appetizing, Early Bird began to fly low over the ground, snooping for some wiggly creatures who were being careless—unafraid because it was so early in the morning. Suddenly he spied a small worm with a strange cocoon on his back and three pairs of silk running shoes upon his feet. The juicy-looking little fellow was picking his way across the hot desert sand. Circling up and away, Early Bird set his sights on the little thing. He was about to dive when the voice like a million waterfalls called from heaven: "Leave Little Worm alone!" Now Early Bird was so hungry and tired that he pretended not to hear the Wonder Maker. He tucked his wings close to his side and started his speedy descent.

At this very moment, Little Worm felt cooler, like a huge cloud was covering the sun. Little Worm glanced upward to see if it was going to rain. He noticed that the cloud had a strange shape, in fact it looked suspiciously like a huge bird. In a flash he realized his enemy had found him. Little Worm stopped dead in his tracks, horrified. There was no bush within reach—no handy hole to pop into out of harm's way; he was a sitting target. He knew there wasn't time enough even to try digging his way into the hard, packed sand beneath his feet. Little Worm was quite sure he would be attacked, and in that long agonizing moment he cried out in terror, "Wonder Maker, Wonder Maker, save me!"

Now the Wind was playing around in the sand dunes a short distance away. The Wonder Maker

reached down with His everlasting arms and hurled the Wind at Early Bird—just as the bird's beak was about to crunch Little Worm's head. The Wind blew the bird off course, and instead of getting a bite of Little Worm, Early Bird got a mouthful of sand. So great was the impact that his beak folded up until it looked like the edge of a saw, fastening him securely in place!

Little Worm fainted and toppled on his back, the six running shoes waving and wobbling in the air. The Wind blew him gently over and over until he rolled under a shrub bush. There he lay quite covered with sand until the Wind wiped the gritty stuff away from his eyes with a cool breath. Little Worm began to cry. "Sh-h-h, sh-h-h," the Wind whispered comfortingly in his little ear. "It's alright now."

Looking up into the clear blue sky they watched Early Bird flying homeward in a really funny zig-zaggy path. After all, it's *very* hard to fly straight when your straight sleak beak is bent!

"See there," said the Wind softly, "he's going home, you're safe no-o-ow! The Wonder Maker saved you. Now let's go on together toward that hill on the horizon. There you will be told what the Wonder Maker wants you to do-o-o-o for Him!"

Talk Time

1. What did the Wonder Maker want the Worker to be 'really' sorry about?
2. Did the weird weed obey the Wonder Maker?
3. Who saved Little Worm from Early Bird?

Prayer Time

Pray that you will not get angry and hurt others.

9
Warm Worms and a Weird Weed

By the time the Wind and Little Worm arrived, the Worker had awakened. He stared curiously at the beautiful leafy vine, which had grown during the night and now covered his booth. "Thank You, Wonder Maker," he exclaimed with joy, "that was so very kind of You. Now I shall be cool all the day long."

The Worker's appetite had returned, so he looked around for something to eat. He spotted some lucious-looking red fruit nestled among the leaves of the leafy vine. He eagerly picked one of the juicy berries and took a small bite. It tasted very, very good indeed. He should have known it would be delicious, for wasn't everything the Wonder Maker made very, very good?

Eating the fruit, which both satisfied his hunger and quenched his thirst, the Worker felt ready for the day. Now he could settle down in the cool shade, his stomach full, and see if the people of Nineveh would get tired of being really, really, really sorry so that the Wonder Maker would have to punish them.

The Worker had not been watching the city long when Little Worm and the Wind arrived. Little Worm looked timidly up at the Worker's face, which still looked dark and cross. *Oh dear,* thought Little Worm. *He hasn't changed yet.*

"Wait awhile," chuckled the Wind, reading Little Worm's mind. "I haven't started on him yet!" The Wind picked up a few handfuls of sand and threw them down on the ground again. He seemed to be practicing for what was ahead. Little Worm looked at the vine towering above him and wondered how such a beautiful vine could grow out of the bleak desert. *Where does it get the water to produce such tempting fruit?* he pondered.

He was just about to crawl under the vine and investigate, when he was met by a delegation of six Warm Worms. Although he had never seen Warm Worms before, he knew immediately who they were because they were all radiating heat—it was like being surrounded by a half dozen little heaters!

Little Worm felt he could do without extra warmth at this point in his adventures, but he was too polite to move away. Instead, he opened the door of his cocoon, brought out the photograph of his mother and father on their wedding day, and began to fan himself with it. The Warm Worms grew very excited and, gathering uncomfortably close, they asked if they could look at the picture. Little Worm didn't want to part with his precious picture, but he handed it to the worm who seemed to be the wisest and hoped he wouldn't get the picture all sticky with sweat!

The Warm Worms gathered around the picture, noting with smiles and giggles the strange clothes their country cousins wore at weddings. Then they took turns telling Little Worm how different their weddings were in Warm Worm Land. Giving Little Worm's picture back to him, the wise-looking Warm Worm invited him to come down below for a hot meal. Since Little Worm was nearly passing out from the heat of the desert, not to mention the added warmth from the little heaters wriggling all around him, he wondered if he could stand it underground. *Surely it will be even hotter down there,* he thought. And *a hot meal—that is the last straw!*

"May I bring my friend the Wind with me?" Little Worm asked the steaming worms, thinking the Wind could sit in a corner and run round and round in circles like a fan. The Warm Worms looked a little doubtful. The Wind looked doubtful too! He'd never been underground in his life and didn't know if he would be able to breathe. "I'd really like him to come with me," pleaded Little Worm, and in the end the Warm Worms and the Wind agreed.

As soon as they all entered Worm Land the Wind started running round and round in circles, trying to catch his breath. The Warm Worms had never felt such a cool breeze before. They laughed and laughed and tumbled out of their homes, dancing up and down in the streets. They begged the Wind to puff harder and harder until he rolled them over. Before long all of Worm Land had turned out to welcome the two strangers. Little Worm couldn't believe the hospitality, but then he had heard once that worms of the desert treated strangers with great courtesy.

A well-dressed worm approached and introduced himself, saying that the Sultan had invited the two visitors to eat a banquet with him in his home. Little Worm glanced at the Wind, who nodded acceptance of the kind offer. As soon as they entered the Sultan's hallowed hole, Little Worm noticed some interesting looking art work on the walls. Book Worm had told him tales of such art, but he had never dreamed he would see it in person or that it could be so cleverly made.

Spiral shapes had been formed from the wet sand, then hauled to the surface for drying before being carried back again and stuck firmly to the walls by Tape Worms. Slugs had traced fine silver markings on them, and then Inch Worms, using paint made from bright desert flowers, had brushed on colorful dots and stripes—at one inch intervals of course! The vivid shapes and colors fairly dazzled the banquet hall.

Everyone had stopped talking. The Warm Worms now crowded around Little Worm, and it became a bit uncomfortable. The Wind breathed a warning into his ear, telling him to be on his guard as he had heard terrible tales about these desert dervishes. But the Warm Worms were not threatening Little Worm. On the contrary, they had become quite silent for a very different reason: Little Worm was glowing again. The farther down into the earth he had traveled, the darker it had become and the brighter he had shone.

Standing now in the middle of the Sultan's banquet hall, his bright light illuminated all the beautiful art work the Warm Worms had never really seen before! Throughout the generations worms like them had worked in this room, hanging the pretty spirals into place. They had used their sensitive antennas instinctively to find just the right place for each shape, and because they had worked in pitch darkness, they had never known how much of the wall they had covered. Until this moment they certainly had not known that this very day the work had just been finished! Not one solitary empty spot remained. The walls were perfectly complete.

The silence in the hall deepened as the Warm Worms turned around and around, gazing at the work of ages illuminated for them for the very first time by Little Worm's glowing light. It seemed to them that the whole room had been planned for a special occasion and a special guest. After many long moments the spell was broken, and the Warm Worms once again looked at their special visitors. Worm after worm began to kneel before them, which was really quite hard to do since it meant getting all their knees to bend to the same time!

"Don't," Little Worm pleaded, "please don't do that." Obviously the desert grubs thought the Wind and he were some sort of gods. Little Worm became very upset indeed, crying out, "I'm just a worm like you are; in fact, I'm the very littlest worm from the whole of my pond! I just happen to glow in the dark, that's all!"

"He's been sent by the Wonder Maker to do His will," offered the Wind, playfully ruffling the hairs on his little friend's head.

"Who is this Wonder Maker?" asked the Sultan, suddenly interested. "We have mostly Moslem mites in Warm Worm Land," he explained, "but we do have one or two believing bugs around who have been telling us for a long time we should listen to the Wonder Maker and worship Him. Come," continued the Sultan, leading the way to a place at the head of his table, "sit at my side and tell me your story and all about the Wonder Maker that you serve. After all, our work on the wall is finished, so this surely calls for a celebration!"

The rest of the Warm Worms scrambled for a seat around the table so they could hear Little Worm and the Wind tell their tale. Little Worm looked around the room in astonishment. All the Moslem mites were sitting cross-legged while the Warm Worms were squatting at a very low table. Little Worm didn't think he could cross all his legs at once like the Moslems! This worried him, because he didn't want to offend them by not following their custom. But he knew it would take forever to cross each pair of legs just right at the same time.

While he was thinking about this, one of the Warm Worm waiters pushed a very exotic-looking cast up to the table. It was decorated in a special way, and even the Worker Worms viewed it with surprise. Nobody could remember working on this one.

"Who made that?" one Warm Worm asked another.

"I really don't know," the second worm answered, shrugging his shoulders all the way down to his toes.

Of course Little Worm didn't really know who had made it either. He was just grateful that he could use the beautiful work of art for a seat, so he prepared himself to enjoy the feast and to share his story.

As they dined the Warm Worms and the Moslem mites listened in solemn silence to all their two guests recounted. Every now and then the Wind would rush to the corner of the banquet hall. Panting, he would run round and round in circles, fanning everyone. Then he would return to the table and put in a word or two if he thought that Little Worm was leaving anything out.

The Sultan listened with great interest and, finally, much, much later when the table was bare, he spoke:

"Little Worm, I believe all that you have told me. Years ago I dreamed about a worm who would come into my home and bring light so that I would be able to understand the deep mysteries of life and death. When your God, the Wonder Maker, sent you to us today and I saw your glow, I knew that you were the messenger I had been waiting for."

Little Worm was so excited he jumped off his beautiful seat, whereupon the thing began to shake all over. Everyone was shocked! As they watched, musical notes jumped from the top of the cast, stretching and singing as they came. The small figures had tiny black faces with just one shiny white eye. Big smiles covered their bodies. They ran around the room and made all the worms join tails and form one big ring. The musical notes pulled Little Worm right into the center of the circle.

Then the mysterious cast, the one Little Worm had sat on, fell flat on the floor, shivering and shuffling itself into a glowing sheaf of papers. The notes, having sung their song of praise, danced onto the paper and arranged themselves into simple words.

The Wind whistled softly, and Little Worm shivered. He knew at once that the words on the paper were his final message. But who could read it to him? Little Worm explained to the Sultan that he had been awaiting the Wonder Maker's instructions and now believed they had been in this room all this time, waiting for his arrival. "Would you be so kind as to read the message to me?" Little Worm asked him.

"I would be deeply honored," the Sultan replied, humbly bowing his head. With Little Worm standing at his side lighting up the heavenly message, he read slowly and with wonder, "Find the seed of the weed."

"What does that mean? Is that all?" asked Little Worm, perplexed.

"Let's go—we know someone who might know," chattered a Warm Worm who was excitedly fanning his red face. So everyone jumped up and tried to squirm out the door at the same time. The Sultan called everyone to order, then he asked Little Worm and the Wind to go first.

Making their way down the winding underground tunnels with Little Worm lighting up the way, everyone eventually came to a cozy cavern where a bunch of very sleepy seeds were tucked in for the night in a seed bed. "Oh," whispered Little Worm, "I hope we won't wake them all up."

"The seeds won't mind," said the Sultan cheerfully. "They didn't expect to see the light of day for a long time, so they will be pleasantly surprised."

It was true. The seeds laughed sleepily and struggled to rub the tiredness from their eyes. "Where's the 'seed of the weed'?" the Sultan asked the Father Seed.

"I don't know what you mean," he answered, rubbing his smooth face.

Then Baby Seed squealed, "Come over here, Little Worm, and bring your bright light with you."

"Just look at that," exclaimed the Wind in wonder. There at the edge of the seed bed was the strangest looking thing anyone had ever seen. The seeds nearby said that they had dreamed in the night that the soil had moved and the strange thing had pushed upward.

The Sultan kneeled for a closer look at the seed. "It's a weed that looks like a vine, I think," he said.

"A vine!" exclaimed Little Worm. "This must be the bottom of the strange and beautiful vine I saw shading the Worker high above us!"

The Sultan again took the Wonder Maker's letter from a servant, who had been carefully carrying it, and read some more words that had mysteriously appeared upon the paper. "Eat it, Little Worm," said the message.

Everyone fell into a wondering silence. "Eat it?" gasped Little Worm. "Whatever does the Wonder Maker mean? I can't . . . I mean I don't . . . well, He must know I'm made to eat pollen, not huge vines that are bigger than a man! I mean, He created me!"

The Wind moaned softly, whirling around the edges of the crowd, wondering what Little Worm would do now. The Warm Worms wriggled around the weird weed, whispering to each other. Little Worm's light dimmed—he was very unhappy. With deep inner certainty he now knew without a doubt that this was the task the Wonder Maker had planned for him from the very beginning. His little heart ached with despair. How could the Wonder Maker bring him all this way, protect him through all his trials and troubles, only to mock him like this? Little Worm grew irritated, angry actually. He thought, with more than a little self pity, *I left my father and mother and Greedy, Grumpy, and Grubby Grub; I risked my life and limb—not to mention Early Bird's vicious attack—to get here, and now I'm supposed to do something that's utterly impossible.* "It isn't fair!" he sobbed aloud. "I can't eat a vine. Even if I wanted to I couldn't."

"Have you ever tried?" asked the voice like a million waterfalls. At the sound of the Wonder Maker's voice, all the Warm Worms and the Moslem mites threw themselves flat on the floor. Little Worm knelt down too, on his wobbly, knobbly knees.

"No, I haven't tried," he whispered, ashamed of his little temper tantrum.

"If you've never tried, how do you know you can't do it?" the Voice asked cheerfully.

Little Worm thought about that. In his mind he saw the colossal vine standing high above his head. Did the Wonder Maker really intend him to eat it—all of it? The whole matter was really quite ridiculous. *Have I misun-*

derstood the Wonder Maker's word? he wondered. Surely He would not ask me to do something that's impossible!

The Wind whispered in Little Worm's ear that the Wonder Maker delighted in taking the ridiculous and turning it into the miraculous. But Little Worm was not convinced. Then he had another thought. *What about the Worker shading himself underneath the vine's cool leaves? He won't be thrilled to bits with me if I gobble up his shelter! Does being obedient mean you have to make someone mad at you?*

But before he even finished asking that question, he already knew the answer. From past experience he knew that everybody isn't always pleased when you do the right thing. He had a nasty feeling about this situation, though. Surely a *disobedient*, disgruntled prophet would be made angrier still if he saw someone else being *obedient*!

"Eat it, Little Worm," insisted the Wonder Maker.

"Eat it—eat it," echoed the Warm Worms in unison.

"But how, how do you eat a vine?" cried Little Worm, his light so low by this time that the cavern was nearly dark again.

"You take the first bite," said the Wonder Maker, calmly.

Little Worm clutched his antennas in his hands and thought and thought and thought. How did he know he couldn't do it if he had never tried? Would the Wonder Maker mock him by commanding him to do something he couldn't do? Surely not. He knew the Wonder Maker was not like that. Then Little Worm made up his mind. He decided he would try. *I have nothing to lose,* he thought; *anyway I can't turn back now. I've come so far already, I can't fail now.*

With each thought of obedience Little Worm's light glowed brighter and brighter. Moving closer to the huge root of the weird weed, he opened his little mouth as wide as he possibly could, and shutting his eyes, clamped his teeth into the root!

"Ah-h-h-h-h-h-h-h," sighed all the Warm Worms, clapping their hands in delight.

Little Worm couldn't believe what happened next. The piece of vine he had bitten off melted in his mouth. It tasted absolutely delicious. He bit into the vine again and again, smacking his lips, chewing through the big root in no time at all. "Wow," he shouted in between gulps, "I never dreamed obedience would taste so sweet!"

His little light shone brighter and brighter until it became a beacon. All the Warm Worms followed him up the crumbling stem, urging him on, laughing and crying with joy. It wasn't long until Little Worm neared the surface of the sand and daylight poked through to meet them.

Then it was all over, and the Warm Worms, Little Worm, and the Wind all popped outside together. With his mouth full of the scrumptuous vine, Little Worm squinted upward into the glare of the midday sun. To his horror he caught sight of the furious face of the Worker sitting beside the broken pieces of his booth, which had crumbled under the weight of the dying vine. "Oh dear Wonder Maker," gasped Little Worm, hastily swallowing his last bite of vine, "*now* what!"

Talk Time

1. Why did Little Worm feel God had been unfair?
2. How do we find out we can do things we don't think we can?
3. What did Little Worm do?

Prayer Time

Pray about doing impossible things.

10
Silk Worm

This time there was no escaping. The Worker's ferocious eyes were firmly fixed upon Little Worm, and it was very clear that the indignant man wasn't one bit pleased with what had happened to the vine! Little Worm felt terrible. Perhaps he had misunderstood the Wonder Maker's instructions. After all, the Wonder Maker had gone to great trouble making the leafy thing grow up in just one night. *Being obedient shouldn't make other people uncomfortable,* Little Worm mused. *It was hard to do what you were told when you were not appreciated!*

The Worker shifted his angry eyes off Little Worm for a moment and surveyed his surroundings. Gone was his booth, and gone with it the shady relief from the fierce sun. A great sadness grew in his heart. He thought of all the hours and energy it had taken to cut the branches from the sparse desert trees to make his booth.

He became even sadder when he looked at the

withered vine, which had been the most beautiful and unusual living thing he had ever seen. Turning his angry eyes back to Little Worm, he decided to use his heel on the destructive creature.

"Stop!" called the Wonder Maker from heaven with the voice like a million waterfalls. "The worm only did what I told him to do. He was obedient!"

"You mean, You told him to smite the vine?" asked the Worker incredulously. Before the Wonder Maker replied, He picked the Wind up and, whirling His eternal arm around in circles, flung the Wind with tremendous force right into a big pile of sand. The Wind shrieked with glee, spinning like a top and kicking the loose sand high into the air. He whirled a pile of sand across the ground, slinging it against the wreckage of the Worker's booth. Laughing uproariously, the Wind then puffed a breeze into the gritty, grimy heap and playfully flicked sand particles into the Worker's face.

The sun was now high in the sky and beating hotly upon the Worker's head. The poor man stood there, a solitary figure in the middle of that barren place, his forehead throbbing from a terrible headache. Little Worm felt really, really, really sorry for him! He could see exactly what was happening. The Wonder Maker hoped the Worker's headache would slip down a little bit until it reached his heart!

This thought had just passed through Little

SILK WORM 131

Worm's mind when the Wonder Maker appeared and sat down beside the Worker's broken booth. He smiled at Little Worm, and Little Worm smiled back, his little body beginning to glow all over again—and it wasn't even dark! The Wonder Maker invited the Worker to join Him and began talking very seriously with him. Little Worm crawled closer to hear the conversation. The Wonder Maker was saying that He thought it sad that His wind, His whale, His weed, and His worm had gladly obeyed Him, but His worker—who had so many advantages over the other humble servants—had not!

"I obeyed You," replied the Worker, sulkily. "You didn't leave me much option!"

"Didn't you ask the men to throw you into the sea?" replied the Wonder Maker. "That would have been the end of you if I hadn't sent My special submarine to bring you back to safety!"

"What would have happened if I had refused to obey You the second time?" inquired the Worker, suspiciously.

"Salvation would have been sent in another way," said the Wonder Maker. "I knew the Ninevites would listen to me, and because I want everyone in the whole wide world to have a chance to be really, really, *really* sorry, I would have made sure they heard My message." The Wonder Maker paused, looking at the Worker tenderly. "But don't you see," He continued, "I wanted *you* to be blessed by being a part of this great miracle. Look," the Wonder Maker said, helping the Worker to his feet by gripping his arm. "Look down there into Nineveh. You can still see the people, and even the animals, dressed in sackcloth, going about their work. Each one of them is of great value to Me. And look at all the children. I created each and every one of those people—one hundred twenty-two thousand of them to be exact! I love them deeply, with an everlasting love. I even love their strange, mangey cattle." The Wonder Maker stopped speaking and threw back His eternal head and laughed and laughed and laughed at the very thought of the funny beasts daubed in ashes and dressed in their sackcloth coats.

Then the Wind and Little Worm understood the great pity the Wonder Maker had in His eternal heart for the Ninevites and for all ignorant people everywhere who had never been told what He required of them.

The Wonder Maker spoke to the Worker again: "You feel sorry for the vine," He said, "for which you have not worked, nor helped make grow—a plant which came up in a night and has now perished. Are not the souls of men, women, and children more important than a vine? Oh, My worker, let Me fan that spark of pity in your heart for the vine into flames of pity for the people of Nineveh!"

The Worker bowed his head. Big tears ran down his

white cheeks, and he rubbed a shaky hand over his forehead, which was lined from the suffering he had caused himself. Little Worm was touched and exclaimed, "Oh, Wonder Maker, is he being really, really, *really* sorry?"

The Wonder Maker smiled gently and nodded. He leaned near the Worker and said something that Little Worm couldn't quite hear. He did catch the last part of it—something about how the Worker should "write all of this down in a book so others could learn from his mistakes!"

Little Worm knew the adventure was all over, and he felt sort of let down. What would he do next, and what would become of him now that the Wonder Maker was finished with him? Perhaps he would just be left to die, since his useful days were gone. He began to whimper and turned to get a handkerchief from his cocoon to wipe his eyes with. He noticed with surprise that the door was open. *How strange,* thought Little Worm, *I can't remember leaving it open.* He peeped inside and gasped. A beautiful bed had appeared, fringed with lovely leaves and embroidered in many pretty colors. The pillows had been made with the petals of a thousand flowers. Soft, warm shafts of light danced about the cocoon in the most inviting way.

Looking more closely Little Worm noticed that the photo of his mother and father on their wedding day was propped against Grumpy Grub's red bandanna on a bedside table. Standing near was a cool sweet drink. Music floated in the air, some sweet melody of praise sung by reeds dressed in lime green whisps of sweet memories. A cool breeze circulated throughout the cocoon, blown by the Wind who whispered "Go-o-o-o-odbye," then disappeared.

Little Worm sighed. He was weary, and it was time to climb into the heavenly cocoon and go to sleep. He wasn't a bit afraid. In fact, he was full to the brim with joy and a sweet contentment! Feeling very, very, very tired, he smiled happily and crawled into the beautiful bed. The Wonder Maker switched off the shafts of light, tucked him firmly under the comforting covers, and kissed him fast asleep.

Night followed night, week followed week, and the cool of the desert winter hushed the rest of the wilderness creatures into slumber. The Warm Worms grew used to the sight of Little Worm's cocoon cuddled into a crevice in a sand dune, and they watched over it lovingly until they themselves grew sleepy and had to prepare for their own long rest. Little Worm slept soundly, unaware of the miracle the Wonder Maker was working in his body.

Time passed and spring came round again. One

day the creatures woke up and wriggled upward to the warm sunlight. The Warm Worms were surprised to see a soft dent in the sand where Little Worm's cocoon had rested. They searched awhile for it, but then decided the Wonder Maker had taken it away—which indeed He had.

Springtime had come as well to Little Worm's Pond, and the creatures there bustled about their work with a spring in their step—especially the frogs! The mother frogs had quite a time trying to keep their children from leaping all over the place. Licky Lizards scampered up the stalks of trailing vines, chasing unsuspecting bugs. Little Worm's Aunt Ethel sat and sunned herself in her reed rocker, enjoying her memories, as old folk will. She thought about Mother and Father Worm and sighed. After Little Worm left on his Great Adventure, they had climbed into their cocoons for a long rest. When they returned they were decked out in stunning new robes. But a terrible accident had happened. An enemy had come to the Pond and gobbled them up. A tear came to Aunt Ethel's eye, it was all very sad; but that's how life was sometimes—*sad*. She had always hoped they would come and live with her in her roomy treetop house. She was often lonely, but she had grown used to being alone and quite enjoyed the peace of her pretty perch.

Aunt Ethel was sipping a cup of dandelion tea when her rocking chair began to sway furiously. *Good-*

ness me, she thought, clinging on for dear life. *What a wind! Wherever is it coming from?* Looking upward, she gasped in surprise. Bits of sand grit and leaves were swirling, and high above she saw a strange round object carried on the wings of the Wind. The thing began to fall her way, and Aunt Ethel hastily fluttered out of her chair and called for the grubs to come and see the strange sight.

Down, down, down floated the heavenly cocoon, for that is what it was, brought safely home to rest in the arms of Little Worm's friends. The Wonder Maker had sent the Wind and his wife, the Whirlwind, to pick the cocoon up at Nineveh and fly it safely to Aunt Ethel in her treetop house.

"I'm sure I've seen this strange thing before," said the old lady butterfly.

"I *know* I've seen it before," shouted Grubby Grub, shaking all over with excitement. "It's Little Worm's cocoon!"

"Open the door, Aunt Ethel!" urged Greedy Grub, the biggest, widest grin imaginable almost splitting his face in two. Even Grumpy Grub was smiling, and he hadn't done that since Little Worm had left.

With a trembling hand, Aunt Ethel opened the door. Peeping inside, she gave a fluttery sort of scream and fainted, falling with a faint thud beside the beautiful bed.

"Why, Aunt Ethel," spluttered Little Worm, waking up with a start. "Is that you?" Struggling out of his cozy bed, Little Worm picked up his favorite aunt and carried her carefully to her bed. Then he ran back to the cocoon to fetch Grumpy Grub's red bandanna to fan her with. Aunt Ethel opened her eyes and asked weakly for a bit of butter. (All butterflies like a bit of butter when they've fainted right away, you know!) Turning around, Little Worm found that his friends were gaping at him, their mouths wide open with wonder. He was still befuddled with sleep, but he was alert enough to realize who they were, and oh, joy, he could hardly believe he was home again. Stepping backwards to take in the sight of all his welcoming friends, he missed his footing and, to everyone's horror, fell backwards off the porch of Aunt Ethel's treetop house!

"Fly, Little Worm, fly," commanded the Voice from heaven.

Fly! thought Little Worm *very* rapidly. *Me? But I'm a worm! Worm's don't fly!* Fast, very fast, on the heels of that frightening thought came the memory of the great lesson he had learned in Nineveh. If the Wonder Maker was telling him to fly, he would be able to fly! After all, he had eaten a giant vine, hadn't he? Surely, after that anything was possible.

Spreading out his wings, which he realized he must have grown during his long winter's sleep, he soared upward on the friendly breath of the Wind, who had been playing about with the high branches of the trees until he was sure Little Worm was alright. The Wind caught Little Worm's wings and playfully puffed him back onto Aunt Ethel's porch again. "I flew, I flew!" Little Worm squealed. "Did you see me?" Everyone was laughing and crying and saying hello and trying to hug and kiss him all at the same time.

All of the pond creatures wanted to hear about his adventures, of course, and so that night the Wise Worms arranged a grand gala for him. A bee was dispatched to buzz Book Worm's house and tell him to be sure and come along for the party.

That evening the story was told. Little Worm missed not a single detail of the Great Adventure, and the pond creatures missed nothing of the wonder of it all. At last they sang a hymn of praise, a glorious "thank you" to the Wonder Maker for bringing the little hero back again. Finally, everyone went home.

Little Worm decided to sleep inside his cocoon one last time. Using his new wings he flew up to Aunt Ethel's treetop house. To his great surprise, he found that the precious cocoon was gone! In its place stood a strangely familiar spiral object, decorated on all sides with silver markings and painted with the soft, sweet paint of pollen. "Why, this is from the Sultan's banquet hall!" gasped Little Worm. A spindly spider was spinning some words over the top of it, and Little Worm shouted for Book Worm and his friends to come and see what he had found.

Book Worm, who had grown wings as well, flew straight in the door, his spectacles with the sunshades trailing on a string behind him. The Spider finished the message, and Book Worm, peering through his glasses, read: "Open it, enjoy it, share it. With love from all your relatives in Worm Land."

Gingerly, Little Worm turned a key sticking from the lock and, after lifting the lid, looked inside. He jumped backwards—presents hopped out, neatly tied and labeled, with only their feet loose. Everyone noticed they had Silk Worm's running shoes on. *They must have found the shoes as they wrapped themselves up inside the cocoon,* thought Little Worm.

The parcels ran to Little Worm's dear friends and began to unwrap themselves amidst lots of giggling. Book Worm's parcel finished untying itself first and handed the learned gentleman a pair of very fine contact lenses, each with the tiniest green sunshade attached to the top. Catching the parcel that was dancing with glee around Aunt Ethel, Little Worm helped her untie the string. "Oh, just look at this, Aunt Ethel," laughed Little Worm, when the gifts were opened. "My friends have sent you a beautiful Eastern yashmak, and it even matches the color of your wings! Let me show you how to tie it round your nose!"

"Why, Aunt Ethel," Grinny Grub teased. "You look

so mysterious!" Everyone clapped their wings, and the old lady delighted them all by wheeling about, dancing an Eastern dance.

Grumpy Grub's gift from the Warm Worms was a bag of darkness, for those times when his head hurt. And there was a can of red dust from Nineveh to paint Grubby Grub's house a nice new color for spring. A huge can of the delicious homemade soup from the market of Nineveh had been sent for Greedy Grub—You should have seen his eyes light up! Two of Wriggly Worm's very best holes had been included for the Wise Worms, now that they were very, very old and could no longer dig their own.

After all the presents had given themselves to Little Worm's friends, the pond creatures went to bed, exhausted from all the excitement.

Little Worm sat for a long time on the porch looking at the stars. Now that he was changed and back home again, he knew a whole new life stretched before him. But he felt a bit sad and lonely. Something was definitely missing, but what, he wondered?

He knew his mother and father were dead, for Aunt Ethel had told him so. A big tear ran down his cheek as he remembered them. But then the Wonder Maker had told him that even though he would not see them again on earth, he would most surely see them later in heaven. And until then he had his precious photograph to remember them by.

Sitting quietly under the twinkling stars, Little Worm was startled by a small sound. Spinning around he caught sight of the prettiest little thing imaginable. Silk Worm had alighted on Aunt Ethel's little porch and was shyly twirling her new wings, wondering how to say hello. Little Worm had missed her at the party but had not dared to ask where she was. He was sure she was married by now—after all, she was far too lovely to stay free so long.

But Silk Worm had not married. She had waited for Little Worm, never giving up hope that he would come back and marry her. She had prayed for him every single day and had spun her dreams into a beautiful wedding dress that she now wore.

"Oh, how gorgeous you are," Little Worm whispered, taking her hand. Silk Worm blushed and squeezed his fingers lightly in return. Turning around Little Worm led Silk Worm to the cast. "See what my friends gave us," he said. "Book Worm read the note. It says, 'Open it,' which we did, 'enjoy it,' which Grumpy, Greedy, Grubby, and dear Aunt Ethel have, and 'SHARE IT!' which *we* will!"

"Share it?" stammered Silk Worm, looking at Little Worm, her eyelashes flickering with coy delight.

"Yes, share it," said Little Worm very softly but firmly. "Will you share it with me, Silk Worm? I love you so very, very much."

She smiled and whispered, "Oh, Little Worm, yes, please!"

And so the Great Adventure ended. Or did it? Perhaps it had only just begun!

Talk Time

1. What does "being appreciated" mean?
2. What was the big lesson Little Worm learned in Nineveh that helped him fly?
3. What lesson have *you* learned from Little Worm's adventures?

Prayer Time

Let's pray about it. . . .